My Father's Legacy

THE 80-YEAR HISTORY OF
HALLADAY MOTORS
and the FOUR OWNERS WHO BUILT IT

Carl R. Halladay, Jr.

CRH
MEDIA
LLC

In memory of my wife
JOANNE

And for my children
SUSIE, SCOTT, and CINDY

Contents

A Special Dedication to Don Williams

WE DISCOVERED OUR MUTUAL LOVE OF MUSIC and performance at our first meeting at the Coffee Cup Cafe in 1964 and immediately became close friends. We would meet for lunch at least once or twice a week. After a few years of arguing about who would pay we finally laminated one of Don's business cards with the words, on the back "My Turn." We passed that card back and forth for the next fifty-plus years.

I started talking about writing this book about fifteen years ago and all through my procrastination Don's standard joke was "Give me a day's notice and I'll write the Foreword."

Unfortunately, he never got the chance. I continued to procrastinate, and Don passed away on November 13, 2019, after a long bout with Parkinson's disease. I would like to have read his foreword. All who knew him knew it would include a tongue-in-cheek joke.

Don was my best friend!

Preface

I BECAME A FULL-TIME EMPLOYEE of Halladay Motors in 1964. I worked very closely with my father, and we attended most meetings together. Whether at a meeting or just having lunch at the Hitching Post Inn, he captivated his audience with his stories about his time at General Motors. Born in 1903, he literally grew up with the automotive industry, and over the years collected many stories about it. On several occasions, I asked him to put those stories on tape.

Finally, between 1968 and 1971, he did just that! In the evening, with his cigar and bottle of scotch, he went to the basement and recorded his life story. He started when he was born and continued through 1944 when we moved to Cheyenne. The recordings were done on an AKAI machine with 7-inch spools of tape. I later transferred them to 15–90-minute cassette tapes. Over 20 hours of first-hand history.

This became a treasure trove of information for me that most writers never enjoy. Most of the direct quotes in this book came from these audio tapes. The recordings, along with many photos and other memorabilia that I had saved, made "My Father's Legacy" a true joy to write.

Carl R. Halladay, Jr.

Moving to Cheyenne

MY FATHER, CARL R. HALLADAY SR. moved himself and his family: his wife Eleanor, Barbara (9), and Carl Jr. (5) to Cheyenne, Wyoming in October 1944. He had spent 20 years with General Motors, 10 years at the General Motors Proving Ground, and 10 years with the Oldsmobile division.

All automobile production ceased during World War II when the plants were converted to producing war material. He had been called back to Oldsmobile's headquarters in Lansing, Michigan to head up the Gun School, teaching instructors on the operation of one of Oldsmobile's wartime products. When it was obvious that the war was winding down, they closed the Gun School, and he was assigned to the Omaha Zone. With a wife and two young children, he had decided to find a dealership location and settle down.

Since his marriage in 1934, he was either traveling or moving to another town. He was spending weeks at a time away from home, calling on dealers. My mother was from Alabama, my sister was born in Jamestown, New York, and I was born in Wheeling, West Virginia.

What brought the reality of all this corporate travel into focus happened after we were settled in Cheyenne. My sister was about to enter the fourth grade and one night at the dinner table my dad asked her how she felt about going to a new school and if she thought she would have any trouble fitting in.

Her reply was: "Daddy, I've never finished at the same school that I started at the beginning of the year."

Choosing a Location

Alfred P. Sloan became Chairman of General Motors in 1937 after serving the previous fourteen years as its president. One of Mr. Sloan's policies at that time was that if any dealer or a family member was called up for the war effort, enlisted, or drafted, General Motors would hold that location open till after the war ended. With the uncertainty of when automobile production would resume, some dealers had already made the decision that they did not want to reopen after the war. These dealership locations became an 'open point'. My father looked at several of these 'open points' from Texas to Florida but he had always had a love for western culture and lifestyle.

Part of his requirement was that he wanted a town large enough that his dealership could properly departmentalize but small enough to be affordable. Cheyenne fit the bill.

Working for Oldsmobile, he had access to all the demographics and business history of the locations he was interested in. When the opportunity presented itself, he did some research and found that Cheyenne had a very stable economy. It had not experienced the ravaging effects of the Great Depression that he had experienced firsthand while working on the East Coast in the late 20s and early 30s.

He discovered that Wyoming's known coal reserves at that time were greater than Ohio, Pennsylvania, and West Virginia's combined. Cheyenne was the capital city with as many federal jobs as state jobs. It was a transportation hub at the crossroads of two major highway systems, coast to coast and border to border, and the main shops on the Union Pacific Railroad. It was also the home of F. E. Warren Army Base.

All provided very stable payrolls. The future was bright.

Our family at the Grand Opening of our first permanent dealership, 408 E. Lincolnway.

Seven Months Earlier

April 1944, my father, working out of the Oldsmobile Zone office in Omaha, was calling on one of his dealers, Frank Haler, in North Platte, Nebraska.

"While I was talking with Mr. Haler in his office, he suddenly said, 'Excuse me' and went to the front door where four well-dressed men had just walked in. After a few minutes, he returned and said,"

"Carl, didn't you tell me that you were looking for a dealership and wanted to settle in the West?"

I said, "Yes, I was."

"Well, one of the men you saw me with was Frank Clark. He was the Oldsmobile, Cadillac, and GMC Truck dealer in Cheyenne, Wyoming. He told me that he had been upset with General Motors for some time and had no intention of staying in the automobile business after the war. Carl, I think that would be an excellent opportunity for you."

Two weeks later my father took a trip to Cheyenne to check things out. It was late April when he left sunny Omaha with green grass and the trees just starting to bloom and by the time he reached Cheyenne, there was brown grass and a full-blown blizzard. He wondered, "What the hell did I get myself into?"

The first person he talked to was Bob Hanesworth at the Cheyenne Chamber of Commerce. Unimpressed with the information available from the Chamber, he asked Mr. Hanesworth if there was someone, he could talk to who had some business knowledge and the pulse of the community.

Bob said: "You might want to talk to Rudy Hofmann. This being Saturday morning you will probably find him at the grain elevator."

Not giving much more information about Rudy, he gave my father directions to the grain elevator.

Upon arriving at the elevator, my dad saw an older man with his feet up on the desk, in bib overalls, reading the newspaper.

My father said, "I'm looking for Rudy Hofmann."

"I'm Rudy," came the reply.

Then my dad gave Rudy his business card and told his story about coming to Cheyenne and looking for property to build his new dealership. Rudy was cordial but didn't have any immediate recommendations. After they visited for a while, he said there was an empty bus garage across from the Union Pacific Depot.

Not having any other prospects, my dad said "I'd like to look at it. Who's the owner?"

"He's a man from Colorado and is in the beer business," Rudy replied.

Before my dad could say anything else, Rudy was on the phone to Golden, Colorado, and said, "Adolph, there's a man here that might be interested in leasing your bus garage."

My dad had no idea who Adolph Coors was and had never heard of Coors Beer.

Arrangements were made with Coors' manager, who was running the hotel in front of the garage, to show him the facility. As it turned out, that space was not a good fit for a dealership.

As he was leaving, Rudy asked: "Have you made any banking arrangements yet?"

The answer of course was no. He had been in town less than a day and Rudy was only the third person he had met. Rudy then suggested that he stop by the American National Bank and gave him directions.

Saturday mornings the banks open at 10:00 a.m. Not familiar

with the town, and the directions being fairly vague, he stopped at the first bank he saw as he was coming down Capitol Avenue. Upon entering, he asked to talk to one of the officers of the bank. The receptionist pointed to a man at the end of the room. My father introduced himself and proceeded to tell him the reason for his visit.

He left after a brief visit and a curt response from the bank officer, who said, "There's a war on and there's no place for a dealership here."

My dad left that bank, Stock Growers, utterly disgusted and proceeded down Capitol Ave., where only a block away, on the opposite side of the street, he saw a sign that said, American National Bank, and immediately thought, "I went to the wrong bank. That's the one Mr. Hofmann was talking about."

As he entered the bank, he was greeted by a receptionist with an entirely different attitude than the one he had just left. He was immediately introduced to Don Wageman, vice president of the bank, Wageman said: "I heard you were in town!"

My father was perplexed at first but later realized that Mr. Hofmann had called ahead.

Once again, he went through his story with Mr. Wageman about his time with General Motors, his plans to open a dealership in Cheyenne, and his search to find a temporary location to operate from.

After thinking for a few minutes, Mr. Wageman said, "How about a filling station with two or three stalls in the back."

"Is there something like that here?" my father asked.

"Yes, I happen to know of a filling station close to the airport at the edge of town that has just changed hands. The Mobile Oil

Co. purchased it and Chief Oil Co., their distributor here, will take over the operation."

"I sure would like to look at it," my father said, and he took the address — 3920 Central Avenue.

When he arrived, they were in the process of taking down the old signs. He rushed right back to the bank and said: "That looks like it would make a good temporary location. Who can I see about renting it?"

Wageman said, "Well, a fellow by the name of Jack Mabee runs the Chief Oil Company, but he's on a job up in Alaska. His father-in-law, who started the company, is looking after the business and his office is right here in this building (the Hynds Building). Let me take you up there."

Don Wageman walked him up, where my dad met Les Miller, a former Governor of Wyoming, who was the father-in-law of Jack Mabee. That was a wonderful entrée.

After explaining his situation to Mr. Miller, they both went to see the building, which Mr. Miller was not familiar with since Mobile had just purchased it.

"I immediately realized that it would be an ideal building for a temporary location," my dad recalled, "and after some serious convincing, he finally agreed to rent me that filling station.

This was our first dealership location in Cheyenne."

Rudolph J. "Rudy" Hofmann owned the Cheyenne Elevator Co. and was in partnership with Dan Rees as a wholesale beer distributor. He was also on the Board of Directors of the American National Bank and would later become President.

Our First Location

3920 Central Avenue, 1944-1945

MY FATHER KNEW THAT THIS LITTLE FILLING STATION would be excellent for a temporary location. The War was still on and there were very few buildings available in Cheyenne, so he jumped on the chance to get it. At first, the owner was reluctant, but my father persisted and finally got him to agree to a month-to-month lease.

It was in a good location on a busy street, North Central, close to the airport and right across from the Owl Inn Restaurant. Although there wasn't any new car production at the time, he was appointed the Oldsmobile dealer for Cheyenne and within a year he obtained the Cadillac franchise.

The Grand Opening was held on November 15, 1944.

During WWII, Cheyenne's airport was home to the United Airlines Modification Center employing up to 4000 workers refitting B-17 Bombers with aircraft armament and other combat systems. As a result, Cheyenne was classified as a 'critical labor shortage area'.

In 1945, Cheyenne was a town of about 25,000, so many of the workers lived in nearby towns, such as Laramie, Wheatland, and Fort Collins, Colorado, and would be bussed to work by United.

My father was confronted with many obstacles in starting his business. He recalled: "There were all kinds of regulations. I had to arrange to get a license to handle gas rationing stamps. I couldn't buy any equipment without a permit. I couldn't sell tires without going to another government agency for approval. These things didn't bother me but the one thing that disturbed me was, I couldn't hire anyone without permission.

"I had hired a filling station attendant from Ogallala, Nebraska before opening the business. Then, after I began buying a few used cars that needed to be reconditioned, I found out, that because Cheyenne was designated a 'critical labor shortage area,' I couldn't hire anybody until I first got permission from the local employment board.

"Ralph Rand, whom I had met, oversaw the board that was

made up of local businessmen. They had to follow strict rules set up by the Federal Government.

"I filled out the application, indicating that I wanted to hire three mechanics.

"In a few days, I got a reply in the mail. It said, 'You are authorized to hire' and there was a blank, and I'll be doggone if there wasn't a zero there. I wasn't allowed, by government edict, to hire anyone other than that one filling station attendant.

"Well, I went down to see Ralph Rand when I got that letter. I was discouraged and furious. I started telling him my story that there hadn't been a dealer here for over two years and I knew how many Oldsmobiles were in the area and that transportation was very necessary for the war effort and people needed transportation and I couldn't understand the board's decision. They won't let me hire anyone!

"I was so upset while I was telling him this, that I broke down and bawled. I couldn't help it.

"He finally settled me down and said, 'I see your point and I'll present it to the board tomorrow night'. And, by gosh, that man, Ralph Rand, came to my rescue and convinced the board to allow me to hire two men, if I could find them."

My father also knew that service and gasoline sales alone would not be enough to cover his overhead. Another government program, the OPA (Office of Price Administration) set the ceiling prices on almost all goods sold during the war, including automobiles. You could sell every used car you could find with an OPA markup ceiling of 25%. He needed to sell used cars, but where to get them?

Due to gasoline rationing during the war, many people, especially in larger metropolitan areas, decided to sell their cars. To build up their inventories, a few Cheyenne dealers elected to send buyers to auctions back east and have the cars shipped back by rail. My father couldn't afford that luxury.

As my father tells the story, "One of my contacts at General Motors was Ralph Morrison. He called and said he was flying back to Detroit from San Francisco and asked if I would like to meet him during his fuel stop in Cheyenne. We met at the airport terminal during his fifteen-minute layover, and I told him about my problem of getting used cars.

After going over a few other suggestions, he asked, 'Have you done any advertising?'

Newspaper advertising back then was fairly expensive and the only ads you saw were for selling cars.

I asked Ralph, "How much do you think I should spend?"

He said, "Whatever it takes."

I spent $40 on that first ad to buy cars, which was a lot of money for me, and to my amazement …it worked!"

"I started getting results almost immediately. What I didn't realize, and neither did any of the other dealers in town, was that we had a built-in market right here in Cheyenne. Right under our noses."

Fort Francis E. Warren Army Base was home to a quartermaster training school. New recruits arrived and, after training, would be shipped to Europe, the Pacific, or other war locations. This was their 'Jumping off Place'. Many of the soldiers had driven to Cheyenne and would sell their cars when they left.

"90% of my used car purchases during those first few years came from the Base. I went from selling 5 used cars a month to over 30. I will forever be indebted to Ralph Morrison."

John Lueras

My father asked the previous service station operator, Ertle Newcomb, if he knew of anyone who could paint a sign for the used car lot.

Ertle said, "There is a young man who works at the United Airlines Modification Center as a painter and mechanic. He might be able to do it."

John Lueras only lived a few blocks from the filling station and would stop in after work to buy gasoline. A few days later, my father hired Johnny to paint the sign and then asked if he would be willing to stop by in his off hours and paint and recondition some of our recently purchased used cars.

Johnny agreed and he began to stop by every day, asking if there was more work. "We would both look the car over and dicker on what he would charge me. Then I'd pay him when the work was done. The volume of cars started to increase, and we were creating a backload. Johnny started bringing in a helper and before I knew it, he had three or four men working for him, sometimes till midnight."

The modification center was winding down and after a few months, my dad convinced Johnny to quit his job with United and come to work full-time. My father often referred to John Lueras as one of the smartest men he knew and said he was a natural salesman. He started as a salesman and progressed to become our general sales manager.

My father recalls, "He was like a sponge, quickly learning everything he could about the automobile business. He also gave me a lot of my gray hairs."

John Lueras was with us for 21 years until he purchased the Oldsmobile-GMC Truck dealership in Laramie, Wyoming in 1966.

The war ended on V-J Day, August 15, 1945. I remember participating in the celebration by honking the horns on every car on the lot. I was 6 years old.

Establishing the Name

WHEN MY FATHER OPENED HIS BUSINESS in Cheyenne there were already 14 new car dealers. Most were only selling one brand of car. Being the "new kid on the block" it was very important that he establish his name.

Cal Holliday had been a well-known businessman in Cheyenne before the war. Holliday had been mayor in the 1930s and had a city park named after him. A few old-timers imagined there was a connection between Carl Halladay and Cal Holliday.

Early on, my father had a steadfast rule with the news media that he would not pay for any ad that misspelled or mispronounced his name.

*The first syllable is pronounced Hal not Hall (HAL*a*day) like the famous baseball pitcher Roy Halladay.*

It became so ingrained that on several occasions if something occurred in Holliday Park, a new announcer often called it Halladay Park.

He contacted every Oldsmobile owner by mail announcing his new appointment as their new dealer and offering complete service for their car. Without any new car production since 1941, these cars would be at least three years old, sometimes considerably older, and would need regular maintenance to keep them running properly. This personal letter along with the newspaper and radio advertisements helped to quickly establish the Halladay name in Cheyenne.

He designed a logo with Halladay in bold block outlined letters with 'today it's' above and 'Motors, Inc.' below. Over the years the logo has gone through several revisions but has always retained the same recognizable bold block letters.

Temporary Quarters

18th Street and Capitol Avenue, 1945-1946

JACK MABEE RETURNED TO CHEYENNE from his job in Alaska and decided that the facility we had been renting for seven months should be used as a service station and not an automobile dealership. Having only a month-to-month lease my father was forced to move.

My father recalls: "This was a real blow to me! Here I was, new to town, my business was just getting off the ground and I was given 30 days to move."

"GMAC didn't have an office in Cheyenne so Larry Tilker, with General Credit, had been handling my retail auto financing paper. I told Larry about my dilemma and that I was desperate to find a location in a hurry. He told me about a filling station downtown that might be available if he could get all the parties to agree."

The station was in the center of town at the northwest corner of 18th Street and Capitol Ave. It was owned by Wm. R. Dubois and leased to Alex Jensen, the Conoco distributor for the area. Mr. Jensen had subleased it to a local mechanic who operated the station and sold a few used cars. After some negotiations, all parties agreed, and Halladay Motors moved to its second location in May 1945.

"We operated out of this facility from May 1945 until we moved to our new building in December 1946," Carl stated.

Before the war, the building had been one of the oldest automobile dealership locations in the city, dating as far back as 1915. Many different makes of cars had been sold there such as Overland, Willys-Knight, and even Cadillac. The corner had been converted into a drive-through filling station at some point.

As it turned out, the downtown location had some benefits. It was only a block from the Post Office and two blocks from the American National Bank and the Plains Hotel, which was the popular 'Watering Hole' at that time.

My dad became acquainted with many of the downtown businesses and local people and started feeling like he was becoming part of the community.

The 18th and Capitol location had a one-car showroom and a four-stall service department but there was no place to store, or display used cars, so he continued to rent a lot adjacent to the

Mobile filling station for several more months. There was also a vacant lot, a block away, which he rented to store any overflow of cars. He remained there till he moved into the new building on East Lincolnway.

When construction started on the new dealership building at 408 East Lincolnway around the first of May 1945, my father signed a lease with Sinclair to operate the adjacent filling station. Early ads stated: "We Never Close — Halladay Super Service Open 24 Hours Every Day For You." There was enough space at the side of the station to display 12 additional vehicles. He moved some of the used cars from North Central to 400 East Lincolnway but still carried out new car sales and service at 1800 Capitol Ave. for another six months. Around this time, we became the US Royal Tire distributor. We operated the first 24-hour AAA wrecker service in Cheyenne from that station.

400 E. Lincolnway

The Durante Building

408 East Lincolnway, 1947-1955

MY DAD MADE SEVERAL TRIPS to Cheyenne during the summer of 1944. He had already made arrangements for a temporary dealership location on North Central Ave. and was scouting out locations to build a permanent facility after the war ended.

In his audio tapes, he describes what happened next. "After looking at a few other properties, I decided that the best location for traffic flow and accessibility would be on 16th Street, known as Lincolnway, and low and behold, while driving east on Lincolnway one day, I saw a couple of houses being demolished, next to a Sinclair Service Station. People at the service station didn't know what was happening but they directed me to their owner, the Crown Oil Company, and I met Ed Leff."

"Ed didn't know why the houses were being torn down either but told me that the owner of the property was Guido Durante, the local Harley Davidson motorcycle dealer, and was operating out of the old C&S Railroad roundhouse. When I said I'd like to talk to him, he gave me directions to the west part of town off 24th Street.

"I walk into this old, dilapidated roundhouse. I saw a few motorcycles in various stages of repair, but no one was around. Then I heard some loud noises and when I went outside, I saw a man hammering away on the roof. It was the middle of April and windy as hell that day. I hollered up and said I'm looking for Mr. Durante."

"What do you want him for," was the reply.

"I want to talk to him."

He said, "I'll be down in a few minutes."

"When Guido finally got off the roof, I told him that I had talked to Mr. Leff at the Crown Oil Company, and he said that you own those lots next to the station on East Lincolnway where the houses are being torn down. I might be interested in buying the property."

"At this time, I hadn't introduced myself or told him what business I was in. Then when I asked what he had planned to do with that property, his answer almost floored me."

Durante said: "Well, after the war's over, and it looks like it's almost over, there aren't enough garage buildings in this town, and I figured I'd put up a garage for somebody."

"I had prior approval from GM's Motors Holding to buy property but leasing a building would free up much-needed capital. This was one of my big breaks.

"I then introduced myself, gave him my card, and to get out of the wind, we sat in the front seat of my car and talked for the next two hours. Guido and I hit it off great.

"We both determined that this would be an ideal location for the new automobile dealership. We couldn't do anything until the war was over, so we agreed to stay in touch and that I would have first right of refusal for that location."

A little over a year after their first meeting, plans had been drawn up and Guido agreed to build the building to my dad's specifications and be the landlord with one special requirement. He wanted to include an apartment over the showroom. The lease, dated January 1, 1947, describes the dealership building and then specifically states: "except the second floor of said building which the lessor reserves for his own use."

My father recalls, "Completing the facility didn't come easy. After the war, building materials were in very short supply. The bricks, for example, came from seven different brick plants. One as far away as Kansas. Also, in normal construction, you would enclose the building before finishing the interior, but I remember that a week before we opened there was no glass in the showroom windows.

"This dealership was the first commercial building built in Cheyenne after World War II. Loren Hancock was the general contractor and Sam Hutchins was the architect. General Motors helped with the latest designs and innovative ideas and when we opened in January 1947 it was immediately recognized as one of the most modern dealership facilities in the Rocky Mountain area."

The Grand Opening and preview showing of the 1947 Oldsmobile and Cadillac models was held on Friday, February 7th. It was attended by City, State, and automobile representatives.

My father recalled: "Without my knowledge, my good friend, Homer Mouer, with Cheyenne Radio and TV Service, recorded the live broadcast of the Grand Opening, on phonograph record blanks." This was a very early recording technique.

My father brought many innovations to Cheyenne from his training with General Motors. One was to provide uniforms for all the service department personnel. No other dealership was furnishing uniforms. White coveralls for the mechanics and shop coats for parts people and service advisers. Each mechanic was issued two sets of coveralls, one to wear and one to take home and clean with his weekly clothes washing. Uniform companies wouldn't come along till many years later.

Employees, 408 E. Lincolnway

Customer Service

Almost any product you buy today comes with a follow-up email, phone call, or letter asking how your purchase experience was and what can be done to improve the service. This was not always the case!

When you purchase a new or used vehicle everyone's happy. Problems come later when you must give up your car, for any reason: regular maintenance, warranty, accident, part failure, etc. People have always demanded individual transportation. They schedule the use of their car and get upset when they must give it up. How these problems are handled can make all the difference in the success or failure of a dealership.

In 1988, Carl Sewell, then owner of the second-largest Cadillac dealership in America, published his book "Customers for Life: How to turn that one-time buyer into a lifetime customer." It immediately became a best seller and a road map for dealers to follow. Many of Sewell's "Ten Commandments of Customer Service" may seem like common sense today but very few of them were in practice seventy years ago.

Long before his book was published, my father had already implemented many of Sewell's practices.

One bit of sage advice I received from my father was: "Your problem is not the customer who complains. In most cases, you can both come to a satisfactory agreement. The customer who experiences bad service, on the other hand, but never complains, is your problem. He just remains silent, but never returns."

A long time ago, way before computers, service repair orders were written by hand. They consisted of a five-page manifold. The first four copies: customer copy, office copy, parts copy, and file copy were on regular paper. The back copy, sometimes called the 'hard copy', was on heavier card stock that stayed with the car and gave the mechanic his instructions.

One day my father realized that there was a lot of blank space on the hard copy. The mechanic didn't need the space used for pricing and accounting. He then got with our forms supplier, Reynolds and Reynolds, and told them he wanted to print a return postcard in that space, complete with return postage. The cashier would attach it to the customer's receipt. It had two simple questions with yes and no boxes. 'Was the work satisfactory?' and 'Do you understand the charges?' and two lines for comments.

This would have been around the early 1950s while we were still in the Durante building. I'm not saying that we were the first ones to follow up this way, but we hadn't seen it before and neither had the Reynolds and Reynolds salesman.

The feedback from these postcards was invaluable. Most would be nice comments thanking us for the service. However, if there was a problem, the service manager would be able to immediately follow up. They didn't have to sign their name. The repair order number was printed on the postcard.

Our commitment to our customers, community, and marketplace continues today.

Service Department, 408 E. Lincolnway

Halladay Motors Philosophy

Our philosophy is to provide our customers with products and services of the greatest value that exceed their needs and expectations — attaining the highest possible levels of customer satisfaction, while at the same time maintaining sales leadership in the marketplace. Assuring continued company profitability and growth. Creating a positive employee environment and fulfilling our obligations to our community.

Tim Joannides, President/General
Manager, January 1994

The Busy 500 Block East Lincolnway

500 East Lincolnway, 1955-1977

IN 1954, THE LEASE ON THE DURANTE BUILDING had a couple more years to go before it would be up for renewal. Guido, I'm sure, wanted us to be there for many years to come but it was obvious, to both of us, that the facilities were not large enough and there was no room to expand. Knowing that he would have to move within the next few years, my father purchased a full city block, which at that time was on the outskirts of town, for a future dealership location.

Roy Manners and David Roush had been in the automotive repair business in Cheyenne for many years and had acquired a Chrysler Plymouth dealer franchise at their location on Thomes Ave. between 17th and 18th St.

After we had been operating at our new location for several years, Manners and Roush purchased some land and began building a new dealership facility just a block away from the Durante building.

They started with a beautiful showroom with slanted windows, but the rest of the building had not been completed. They serviced cars in a Quonset-style building next door until they could finish the service department building.

They had only been operating in this location for a couple of years when they suddenly closed their doors. We may never know the reason why they closed, but the building stayed vacant for close to a year.

The listing Realtor approached my father several times to consider purchasing this single-use property, but his reply was always the same. He had purchased a full city block east of town where he was going to build a new dealership and wasn't interested.

Finally, in desperation, the Realtor, and I'm sure the bank, said they would consider any offer. My father made one that he was sure they wouldn't accept. But they did. And so started our 22-year journey creating "The Busy 500 Block East Lincolnway."

P.S. In a strange turn of events Manners-Roush Motors, a few months later, opened their Chrysler-Plymouth dealership in the Durante building.

Showroom at 500 E. Lincolnway

Our Grand Opening was held November 3, 1955, featuring the new 1956 Oldsmobile, Cadillacs, and GMC Trucks. The move to the new location doubled our space and we grew to 51 employees.

One of the main attractions of the new building was the four-foot-high neon OLDS letters with Cadillac, and a rocket shooting up on the front side. That along with the slanted showroom windows made Halladay Motors one of the most distinctive buildings in Cheyenne.

In 1967 General Motors embarked on a corporate identity program requiring every dealer in the country to replace their existing signs with standardized ones. This required us to remove our iconic neon Olds, Cadillac, and Rocket (shown on the cover) with their plastic panel signs. The building never looked the same since. Oh well, that must be progress.

Changing the sign

Tom Ourada

Fresh out of the Navy, Tom Ourada was hired to work in the parts department at Halladay Motors in 1947. Shortly after moving into our new dealership at 408 E. Lincolnway, we became a US Royal tire distributor. The tires were sold out of the adjacent filling station that we were operating. My father put Tom in charge of the tire sales.

When we moved to our new dealership location at 500 E. Lincolnway, he leased and eventually purchased the adjacent Chevron service station and put Tom in charge of both the service station and tire sales. Business kept growing and several years later we had more need to expand our used car lot than to operate a filling station.

In 1961, Chevron had just built the largest service station in Cheyenne on the northeast corner of 16th St. and Warren Ave. and was looking for someone to operate it. My father made a deal with Tom that he would help him acquire the lease on that station and finance the tire inventory so he could get started in business. This was the beginning of Tom Ourada's long successful career as 'Tom The Tire Man'.

Outdoor Showroom

Childers Manufacturing of Huston, Texas had developed an outdoor showroom canopy for automobile dealers. They had been very popular in places like California and Texas, but we were the first dealership in the Rocky Mountain area to install one. The structure, with its attractive design, immediately changed the image of the entire block.

Fluorescent lights meant you could shop for a used car at our outdoor display any time day or night, during or after hours. Salesmen were enthused by the fact that the cars were cool and inviting for the customer to sit in, rather than the oven-like feeling of getting into a car that had been sitting out in the sun. We built the canopy in 1963 and it immediately set our Used Car Lot apart from every other lot in the city.

Used Car Lot at Night

Bowlerama

AFTER WE MOVED TO THE NEW DEALERSHIP facility at 500 E. Lincolnway, my father was left with a vacant block at the east end of town that he had purchased with the intention of building his new dealership when his lease with Durante was up. The full city block was located between the new KFBC-TV building and Millers Super Market. The story is best told by the following article taken from the first Cheyenne Bowler newsletter dated December 1958.

America's No. 1 Participating Sport Hits All-Time High in Cheyenne With the Advent of Wyoming's Newest and Largest Bowling Lanes — Bowlerama

"November 10th saw the completion of 24 of the finest lanes and complete facilities that may well be the envy of all bowlingdom.

Carl Halladay can take the lion's share of credit, for it was six years ago in 1952, that he bought the location with the intention of building a new Auto sales and service facility. In 1955, Halladay purchased the building that they now occupy, which led Al Sandahl a year later to suggest to Carl Halladay that the East Lincolnway block be used for a much-needed additional bowling facility. Later in 1957, Halladay took an extra week after the National Auto Dealers Convention in Miami during which time he visited several bowling lanes, giving him a new conception of the sport.

Al Sandahl, 22 years in the Neon sign business in Cheyenne, covered the Western half of the U.S. visiting and installing signage at numerous bowling installations.

The tremendous insight of both Carl and Al from these various visits manifested itself in the design of the Bowlerama.

Al Sandahl, with the able assistance of his business partner George Stavropoulos, is now leasing the building and grounds from Carl Halladay. A complete staff of approximately 30 people rounds out the establishment, giving Cheyenne a truly magnificent advancement in the entertainment sport of bowling."

Bowling, like my dad would say, "took off like gangbusters!" The business was booming, which didn't go unnoticed by the two managing partners. A group of investors was assembled and after four years of operation, Al and George exercised a clause in the lease agreement that allowed them to purchase the land and building.

My dad envisioned being part of the bowling business for many years and had even pursued obtaining a liquor license but that was not to be. He was still very proud of his contribution to this very successful part of Cheyenne's entertainment industry.

Bowlerama Groundbreaking — My father, in a suit jacket and Al Sandahl holding shovels. I am the first one kneeling on the left.

Westland Road — Motor City

2100 Westland Road, 1977 – Present

IN 1976, FRANCIS FERGUSON AND MICK CHEESBROUGH bid
on and purchased 60 acres in west Cheyenne from the General
Services Administration. When I-25 was completed on the west
edge of town, several years earlier, it isolated a parcel of land
between the interstate and the C&S Railroad line. This land had
previously been part of Warren Air Force Base. Francis and Mick
formed the Westland Development Corp. and sold the first parcel
to Fassett-Nickel Ford.

When Jack Fassett and Nick Nickel purchased Walton Motor Co. it was with the understanding that they would build a new dealership facility. Tyrrell Chevrolet had moved to West Lincolnway several years earlier and when we opened at the end of 1977 the three of us accounted for over 80% of Cheyenne's automobile business. Within a year, Leo Payne Toyota, who had been renting the Durante building downtown, built a new dealership facility on Westland Road. That's when it really became 'Motor City'.

Build Team Groundbreaking — L to R: Noel Griffith, Bob Clary, Carl Jr., Carl Sr., Mick Cheesbrough, Larry Martin

Construction

On September 9, 1977, a luncheon of over 20 people from auto representatives to contractors and local news media was held at the Hitching Post Inn to introduce the new Halladay Motors facility. It preceded the official groundbreaking ceremony at the dealership location. Cheesbrough, Clary & Associates was the contract management firm. Noel Griffith was the architect and Larry Martin was the Engineer.

Many innovations and the latest technology were incorporated into the design and construction of our new dealership facility. The prestressed concrete structure by Stanley Structures used insulation-filled hollow-core walls and "twin-tee" roof members. Decorative aggregate fascia and columns encompassed the showroom and elevated patio display area. The outdoor display area would accommodate 18 new vehicles in addition to six cars displayed inside the showroom. The use of prestressed concrete cut construction time by about 40 percent.

The service department and body shop both used a tandem-stall arrangement creating an additional one-third more usable productive space under roof while improving mobility and traffic flow. Another major innovation was that the entire building was heated by a gas-fired boiler eliminating the need for individual unit heaters and separate forced air systems. Also, a considerable number of skylights were utilized throughout the building to help further conserve energy.

The Grand Opening was held on June 23, 1978.

Within a few years of moving into our new dealership facility and with a vision of future expansion, we purchased the adjacent 5 acres of vacant land. It was an odd pie-shaped lot with minimum frontage on Westland Road. It was further compromised by the fact that Westland Development had carved out and sold a small parcel to Phil Habercorn for his Cheyenne Tent and Awning business. We eventually purchased that property from Phil and the building was converted to the Halladay Motors Accessory and Detail Center. A small office building was placed on the lot, and we established a separate Truck Sales Center.

As it turned out, many years later, this property proved to be an ideal location for the new, state-of-the-art Subaru dealership.

Carl R. Halladay, Sr.

Early History

Carl Halladay was born August 17, 1903, to Joseph and Fannie Halladay, on a farm outside the small town of Bradford, Ohio. He was the youngest of four children. They were members of the Church of the Brethren, a fundamentalist church but not nearly as strict as others in the area such as the Quakers and the Old Order Amish.

Carl recalls, "We would attend church three times a week, Wednesday evening and twice on Sunday. My whole social life growing up revolved around the church.

"I had many chores growing up on a farm. From the very early age of four or five, I milked cows and rode old Grace, our big gentle draft horse, to harrow the fields. I also rode Grace to the one-room schoolhouse about a mile from home.

"My father was very progressive and forward-thinking," Carl recalls, "always looking for new and modern ways to make money."

With farms rapidly becoming mechanized with tractors, his father traveled the county selling manufactured fertilizer to replace what their horses and cows had previously supplied.

He also sold an acetylene light plant for home use. "They were manufactured by the Gem City Light Co., Dayton, Ohio. There would be a central generator in the basement, like a large miner's lamp, where you would mix carbide and water to generate gas that would be piped to lamps throughout the house. We had the first indoor gas lights in our county. This, of course, would soon be replaced by the electric light bulb.

"When I was 8 years old, my father decided to retire and turn the farm over to my sister Estella and her husband Homer Detrich. They had ten children. My brother Les had married and was living on a farm adjacent to ours. My brother Jerry was married and living in Greenville, Ohio.

"My parents then moved into town, Greenville, Ohio, 7 miles from the farm. They bought four acres right across from the Darke County Fairgrounds. I was the last one living at home and still going to school. The land was large enough to have one cow for milking and one horse for pulling the buggy.

"Shortly after moving to town, my father got very ill. Over the next three years, he had several operations but when I was 11 years old, my father died in misery from skin cancer."

Summer Jobs

My dad's first experience at an automobile dealership happened when he was 11 years old. His older brother, Jerry, was working as a sales manager for the Oakland dealer in the nearby town of Sidney, Ohio, and he hired young Carl to grease cars.

"I loved everything mechanical, and this was my dream job. I didn't even care if I got paid." He worked there that summer and the next and lived with Jerry and his family.

The Oakland dealer had traded for a small one-cylinder belt-driven Pope motorcycle.

"As I look back, I don't think that in my lifetime I wanted anything more than that little motorcycle and by golly, with some reluctance, I convinced my mother to let me have it. I took my wages from working at the dealership to pay for it. It was small enough that I figured, even at eleven years old, if it fell over, I could lift it back up. Finally, it came time for me to go back to Greenville and go back to school.

"I remember this so vividly; I left early in the morning, and I was all day going those 22 miles back home. It would run a little while and get too hot or something else would happen. I was very familiar with it because I had already taken it apart and put it back together several times."

As a young boy interested in mechanical things; he thought that little motorcycle was the greatest thing in the world. He loved it.

"After the second summer working for my brother, I got a job with a local bakery driving a bread delivery route while going to school. The Metzger family had a wholesale and retail baking company and had customers throughout the county. By now I am 13 and with my driving experience, they hired me to deliver bread and rolls in their Willys-Overland pickup truck.

"I would get up at 4 o'clock, go to the bakery, and roll buns for an hour and a half before making in-town deliveries to restaurants and grocery stores, all before going to school at eight. Then I received permission from my teacher to leave school an hour early at 3:00 so I could make the 40-mile delivery run to the outlying customers. I would make that run, 80-mile roundtrip, every day during that entire school year.

"The next summer I learned about a new bus company in town with a route between Greenville and Dayton, Ohio, that was looking for drivers."

Back then there were no age restrictions on driving an automobile. His experience at the Oakland dealership and the daily bread deliveries fully qualified him to be a chauffeur and carry passengers for the bus company.

"I would make two round trips a day. One in a 7-passenger Chevrolet FB, which I loved driving, and the other in an International bus. I never liked the International. It was a rattle-trap. I would pick up any passenger, anywhere between Greenville and Dayton and collect money on the rate schedule. I drove that whole summer and as I remember, got paid $30 a week. I was 14 years old."

Joined the Army

"It was my second year in high school, and I wasn't getting along with my mother. I knew then that I didn't want anything to do with farming. I was 16 years old and thought I knew everything, so when a boy from our town, five years older than me, said that he was going to join the Army, I asked if I could go along. I withdrew all my savings from the bank, $26.00, and the two of us took the train to Cincinnati."

"We saw a Staff Sergeant in a booth outside of the Post Office, filled out the paperwork, and were told to report to the recruiting office in the morning.

When we arrived at the office a Major asked me "How old are you?"

"Right then I knew I was in trouble. I had given all the correct information, my name, address, and my mother's name."

I said "18."

He said, "We've checked your record and you're not 18, you're 16 and I'm sorry son but we can't accept you."

"When I left his office, I never was lower in my life."

"My friend got in, but I was totally rejected. As we were walking back to the hotel, we ran into the same recruiting sergeant from the day before and told him my story.

Then he said, 'Stick around another day. Maybe we can fix this up."

"We looked him up the next morning and he said, "I'll tell you what to do. I got it all set up for you, but you've got to remember this. You're 21 years old, and remember, you were born in 1898. If you're 21 then they can't question you."

"Well at the time I was a little leery of doing this and we talked about it all day. I finally decided to go ahead and the next day we went to the recruiting office and there was the same Major."

"He didn't recognize me, I'm sure on purpose because he's trying to get recruits."

The Major asked, "How old are you?"

"'21,' I replied."

"And when were you born?"

"'1898.' And before the day was over, we were at Fort Thomas, Kentucky, getting our uniforms.

"As soon as I got to Fort Thomas, I wrote a letter to my mother.

"Well now, she had already been alerted and knew where I was because they had checked with her the day before.

"I told her that I was already sworn in, and I wasn't coming home.

"I had been there about a week, and right after they dismissed us from a drill, I looked up and there was Rudy Bittner, our next-door neighbor from Greenville. My mother had sent him to check up on me. We had a nice visit and I told him that I didn't want to go home, and if I had to leave and go back, I would run off again. I really wanted to be in the Army.

"He took that message back to my mother and apparently, she was convinced of it. That was the last I heard of it, at least for a while.

"After Fort Thomas, my group went to Camp Grant, Illinois and then we were transferred to Fort McDowell, Angel Island, California. I was assigned to the 15th Infantry and registered as a truck driver. I wanted to get as far away from home as possible, so I had signed up to go to Tientsin, China. The year was 1919.

"The Army finally caught up to me and found out that I was underage. I had to watch my fellow recruits board the transport ship to China while I was left in an empty barracks, awaiting my discharge. After a few days, I talked to an officer who said there might be a way to solve my dilemma. He told me that if my mother would give permission and send my birth certificate in a letter to the Adjutant General in Washington DC, I might be able to stay in the service.

"Well, I did just that. I sent my mother the instructions and finally, after four months, got clearance from the Adjutant General's office with official notice that I am now permanently in the Army for my four-year tour. My mother actually followed through and came to my rescue.

"While waiting at Fort McDowell to learn my fate, they put me to work in the office, filing and making up sailing lists. I saw a build-up of troops in Hawaii, and after receiving my mother's blessing and clearance from the army, I requested and got orders for the motor pool, 11th Field Artillery Brigade at Schofield Barracks, Hawaii.

"Within a few weeks after arriving in Hawaii, when they found out about my driving experience, I was assigned to the Brigade Commander as his personal chauffeur.

"Colonel T.N. Horn was a crusty old cavalry officer. Even though his rank was Colonel, he was filling a General officer position as Brigade Commander.

"I was instructed to be at his quarters at a quarter to eight sharp every morning. The Colonel's horse orderly, Sergeant Red Bardella, would be there at the same time. Red would be sitting on his horse and leading the Colonel's horse.

"Red stood at attention holding the horses' reins and I stared straight ahead in the driver's seat of the car. We never knew when the Colonel came out his front door, whether he would go to the horse or the car. If I heard the back door open, I knew he was taking the car. Not a word was spoken, I would just start driving. This was the strict Army discipline in those days. A good life lesson for me at 17 years old.

"One evening", my father continued, "when we arrived at his home, Col. Horn remained in the car.

"He said: "Halladay, I need a chauffeur for my personal use. Would you be interested, in your off times, to drive my personal car for Mrs. Horn?"

"I said I would, and he arranged for me to get a chauffeur's license. Mrs. Horn played golf in Honolulu about once a week. Many times, after I dropped her off, I would spend the next four hours at Waikiki Beach. This, along with other trips and shopping, opened up a whole new world for me. In my 14 months there, I saw almost everything there was to see on the island of Oahu.

"After I had been in Hawaii for about a year, I started getting very homesick. The talk from my buddies around the barracks was about figuring out how they could get out of the Army.

"One day the company clerk told me: "Your father is not living, and your mother is all alone and needs your help at home. You could get out on Section 29.

"I didn't know what Section 29 was but later learned that there was an Army regulation that you could be discharged from the service, even if you had enlisted for four years if you could prove that you were needed at home.

"I knew that I wasn't going to make the military a career and my real motivation was to get back home and finish my high school education. The company clerk wrote the application letter and the instructions, and I mailed them to my mother. My mother then sent another letter to the Adjutant General in Washington DC. It took about three months before I got the news that I was up for discharge and another week before it was approved.

"When I was about to be discharged, Col. Horn approached me and offered to help me finish my high school education in Honolulu and then recommend me for West Point. It was a wonderful offer, but the Army was not for me.

"I was discharged from the Army on July 26, 1922, on a Section 29 Dependency Discharge."

Dad Woodruff

"When I got out of the Army, I finished High School. I studied hard. I went to one full year and two summer schools and got my diploma.

"My interest in engines and all things mechanical drove my desire to go to college and study mechanical engineering. I found out that my mother couldn't help with any of my college expenses. I had always thought that she was secure but found out later that she was just barely getting by. It was at this time that I found out that my grandfather had set aside just under $2,000 for me. This was my only inheritance, but it was enough for me to start college.

"I enrolled at Ohio State University. That first summer a friend of mine, Howard Lambers, and I got jobs on the railroad in the yard dismantling coal cars. It was hard work knocking out rivets with a 60 lb. air hammer and making sixty cents an hour. I thought that was pretty good.

"Friends of ours from back home had a son who had just graduated from OSU. He financed his way through school by working as a cook for an old bachelor. The house was just across the street from the university. They recommended me to take his place and I got the job. I had never taken much interest in cooking, so my mother had to teach me how to cook and fry and I even learned how to bake bread.

"Dad Woodruff was a roly-poly bachelor who had never married and was well-to-do. He had made his money in mining in Mexico and South America. He was the adult leader for the Masonic youth fraternity, DeMolay, for the state of Ohio, and thus the name Dad. His full name was Charles W. Woodruff.

"He also had a live-in chauffeur, a medical student that he had already hired. So now I'm the cook for Dad Woodruff, living in his big house and making three meals a day for the three of us."

"Now! You don't think my mouth was watering. Dad Woodruff had a twin-six Packard Roadster, one of the finest cars built at that time. I was just the cook, and the medical student (can't remember his name) couldn't care less about what he was driving. Yes, I was jealous, but I didn't say a word.

"I didn't even get to go shopping. Dad Woodruff and the chauffeur would go to the store about twice a week and bring home the groceries in a bushel basket. Then I would put the vegetables and meats in the ice box and the bread in the cupboard.

"One evening, Dad turned to the chauffeur and said, "Didn't we get some cheese on our last trip?"

"Yes, we did" he replied.

"Then Dad looked at me and I said: "Oh, that cheese! You know I opened that package, and it was spoiled badly. It was all green and moldy and I threw it away."

"Then Dad started laughing and laughing, his big belly shaking and when he finally got control, he said, "That was Roquefort cheese and it's supposed to look that way."

"Growing up on the farm, I had never seen Roquefort cheese. Oh well, another life lesson."

Co-op Student

The next year, the money his grandfather had left him had run out. Determined to continue his education, my father did some research and learned about a co-op program offered by the University of Cincinnati. This program allowed you to work your way through college.

You would work for two weeks and then switch places with another student to attend classes for the next two weeks. He enrolled in the mechanical engineering department for that program in 1923. His first work assignment was with a machine tool manufacturing company, the J.A. Fay-Egan Co.

Carl recalls: "I got a lot of experience working with lathes, shapers, and drill presses. I was working 10-hour days earning 30 cents an hour. I had joined the Triangle Fraternity, a national fraternity of engineers, and was living at the house. The $21.00 a week was enough to pay for my room and board.

"Right after I started my second year, I saw a notice on the bulletin board listing a competitive exam for a civil service job at McCook Field in Dayton, Ohio. I was getting tired of the monotonous routine of the machine shop and thought this would be a better work opportunity and it qualified under the University's student co-op program. During your second year, you would work for a month and attend school the next month. I registered, took the test, and lo and behold, out of one hundred applicants, I was one of two students awarded the contract. I was awarded extra credit for my time spent in the Army.

"Now, the next year, without any reservation, was the most interesting and formative experience in my life, insofar as training and learning were concerned, working at the Power Plant Laboratory, Engineering Division of the Army Air Service.

"I worked on many engines in the lab, all experimental, from the barrel engine that developed 400 HP to the inverted Liberty Engine so the pilot could see over it. I loved engines but I also wanted to fly so badly.

"By this time, I was making $125.00 a month, not 30 cents an hour, so I had some extra money to spend. I started to take flying lessons for $5.00 at Lunken Airport in nearby Cincinnati in an Aeronca C-2 aircraft, on the weekends. I wish I could have continued and gotten a pilot's license, but with my work and school schedule, I finally had to quit."

My father was working at McCook Field when Igor Sikorsky was testing one of his first helicopters. He recalls, "I saw the flight. It didn't last long. It went up about 20 feet and fell back down and broke all to pieces, but it was a beginning." He remembers seeing a young test pilot on the base, Lt. Jimmy Doolittle. He also spent many hours working on the development of the Wright J-5 radial engine, the engine that would eventually power the "Spirit of St. Louis" and Charles Lindbergh on the first Trans-Atlantic flight.

Then, after working a year and a half at the Dayton Engineering Laboratory, he was informed that there was going to be a Reduction of Force and his government-sponsored civil service job was going to be eliminated. His co-op status with the University of Cincinnati would continue, but he would have to find another job.

Despite having to leave his job at the laboratory, he would always cherish the memories of his time spent in Dayton at the dawn of aviation history.

General Motors Proving Ground.
Carl kneeling on the right closest to the car

GM Proving Ground

A few weeks before Carl's civil service job ended, his boss, Mr. Insley, called him into his office and said he had just come from an SAE (Society of Automotive Engineers) meeting and heard that

General Motors had recently purchased land outside of Detroit and was just completing the first phase of an automobile test facility. He also said that they were looking to hire some young engineers. Insley wrote to O.T. 'Pop' Kreusser, Director of the GM Proving Ground, and recommended my father and one other engineering student from the laboratory, for the job.

In his bestselling book "My Years With General Motors," Alfred P. Sloan, President of General Motors recalls, "Cars then were being tested on public roads, and there was no easy way of telling whether the test driver had pulled up at the side of the road, taken a nap, and then driven faster than the test schedule called for to make up the necessary mileage. Once one of our engineers discovered a test car jacked up outside a dance hall with the engine running up the required mileage on the odometer. The most important step we took to standardize and improve test procedures was the establishment in 1924 of the General Motors Proving Ground."

Continuing his education as a co-op engineering student, Carl was hired and went to work in June 1925 at the new General Motors Proving Ground at Milford, Michigan as one of their first test drivers.

The beautiful Tudor-style clubhouse on the grounds was underused in the beginning so he and seven of his fellow single engineers were allowed to live in this magnificent clubhouse for the unbelievably low price of $7 a week — room and board.

Carl recalls, "There were always a few vacant rooms reserved for corporate executives on their overnight stay at the proving ground. It was not unusual at that time to have a community bathroom at the end of the hall. Here I am, a young engineer, making $125 a month and I remember, on at least a half dozen occasions, I would be shaving next to Alfred P. Sloan, the president of General Motors."

His first few years were spent in the Technical Data Section with the responsibility of evaluating all makes of automobiles. They would run them through a series of 127 tests.

"We not only tested our products but that of our competition too, both domestic as well as many automobiles from all over the world."

General Motors was very interested in the rapidly expanding automotive manufacturing in Europe. They purchased Vauxhall Motors in Great Britain in 1925 and Adam Opel, the German automobile company, in 1929.

"We tested all these vehicles. They would ship the cars by rail, partially disassembled, in crates. When they arrived at Milford, four miles away, we would assemble them, fill them with fluid, and drive them to the proving ground.

"Opel made everything from a very small, 4-cylinder 4 HP car, the tiniest car I had ever seen, to one that was larger than our Cadillac. They also manufactured a full line of trucks.

"We tested everything from some very bad cars to the very best. The Czechoslovakian Constantinesco could have been the worst. It had what is known as an IV (infinitely variable) transmission. It was nothing more than two flywheels, perpendicular to each other. The face of one flywheel would contact the edge of the other one and by moving back and forth it would change the ratio and speed of the vehicle. It was completely unsatisfactory and gave us nothing but trouble during our tests.

"The best cars were the Daimler, Mercedes-Benz, and Bentley

cars. The most unusual car I drove at the Proving Ground would have to be the 1927 Phantom I Rolls-Royce. General Motors of Canada ordered the car from Rolls-Royce, and we got a six-month permit to take it to the proving ground to check it out. It was a very large car with a wheelbase longer than a Cadillac and very high. It had to be 7 feet tall. Back then, you ordered the chassis, only one was available at that time and then ordered the body from one of four or five different bodybuilders. I remember the chassis cost $16,000 and the body was $9,000. $25,000 in today's dollars would be $435,000.

"J.P. Charles, a fellow engineer, and teammate, and I were given the task of running a series of tests on this car. That was quite an experience, and it took us about six weeks. I learned some interesting things about Rolls-Royce. Their engineering, at that time, was antiquated, old-fashioned by our standards. The steering apparatus, for example, was just so simple in design that if you hit any pebble on the road, you would get a terrible shock in the steering wheel. Well, that had been corrected years ago and incorporated by most automobile manufacturers in this country.

"Now, on the other side of the coin, the precision craftsmanship was unrivaled. One example is the cylinder head was fitted to the block so well that it was completely airtight and compression-proof without having to use a gasket. Up till this time, I had never seen a cylinder head without a gasket.

"Some other odd things about the car, the hood was locked. It had a lock on each side of the hood. Why (chuckle) I don't know. They didn't want anyone in there unless they were authorized.

"I also remember a little anecdote that O.T. 'Pop' Kreusser

said. Remember he was the one that hired me at the Proving Ground. He had gone to Oshawa Canada to pick up the car and as they were checking it out, a Rolls representative came over and said, "I'm sorry Mr. Kreusser but we won't be able to release the car to you today."

"Kreusser asked: "Why?"

"The Englishman replied, "We don't have the proper lubricant. The transmission fluid was not shipped with the car, and we must have our own fluids in the car.

"Kreusser replied, "Now just a minute sir. I have a very busy schedule and I plan to leave this afternoon. What's so special about this transmission fluid?"

"Oh," said the Englishman. "We never allow our cars to be operated with anything but our Rolls-Royce branded lubricants."

"Kreusser explained to the Englishman that he happened to be a chemical engineer and very familiar with their transmission. "It's no different than an American one," Kreusser said, and finally, after about twenty minutes, the man broke down and admitted that it was nothing more than what we call 600W.

"We got the fluid locally and got back to the proving ground that day.

"This is the way that the Rolls-Royce people have built up their product as the finest in the world. If anything goes wrong, It must be because it was mistreated, or someone used the wrong lubricant, or something else. It could never be the fault of the product.

Cadillac V-16

"It was shortly after the first of the year, January 1929, J.P. Charles and I were looking for something to do one weekend so Saturday night we drove to Ann Arbor to a picture show. We arrived back at the Proving Ground after midnight. As we were walking to the clubhouse I said to J.P., "There's a light on and someone is working down there in the dynamometer room. Let's go see who it is."

"And my god, here's Jack Gordon and Fred Arnold with the darndest Cadillac we'd ever seen. It was a standard cab, but the hood was half-again longer than any I'd ever seen before. We knew them both very well even though they didn't live at the Proving Ground. Each division had its own engineering facility in their headquarter city. Jack and Fred worked at Cadillac in Detroit.

"They were running tests on their experimental V-16 engine. They had driven out after dark, thinking everyone would be asleep and they could do some tests and return to Detroit without being noticed. Well, we caught them in the act, and they showed us what they were doing."

In 1926, Lawrence P. Fisher, Jr., President of Cadillac, hired Owen Nacker who had been investigating the possibility of building the ultimate multicylinder engine, a V-16 while working at Marmon. This was exactly what Fisher had in mind for Cadillac. During the next four years, the engine was developed with a level of secrecy more befitting a new military aircraft than a car.

"Our visit with Jack and Fred was almost a full year before they finally got the Cadillac V-16 into production. It lasted eleven years, from 1930 to 1940 but they only built 4,076. I did a lot of work with the V-16. It was a good car, but it just wasn't practical.

It was way too expensive, and you couldn't get enough horse-power for sixteen cylinders. It was also one of the heaviest cars ever built, with models that weighed up to 6,600 pounds."

John F. 'Jack' Gordon went up through the ranks becoming General Manager of Cadillac in 1950 and then elected to succeed Harlow Curtice as President of General Motors in 1958. Fred Arnold remained with Cadillac and retired as Chief Engineer.

Sales Activity

"After I had spent about three years as a co-op engineering student, I was having real difficulties with my finances. I had to decide to either drop out for a year or just quit college. About the time when I was trying to make that decision, the Proving Ground established a new department called the Sales Activity.

"Well, I had the opportunity to join this department, which appealed to me. I confided in my bosses in the GM building, and they agreed, and that's when I moved from spending three years in the technical data section to the new Sales Activity, GM Proving Ground. I never went back to school. I was now involved in sales. I was always a 'people person' and as I look back, I would have made a lousy engineer. A sheepskin (diploma) didn't mean as much back then as it does today.

"My new boss was Walter Wright and later Hamilton "Ham" Newman, both headquartered in the GM building in Detroit.

"The reason this department started was just a matter of evolution. There were a lot of inquiries from all over the world from General Motors people who wanted to see this new and unique proving ground. At this time there were 27 assembly plants operating outside of the United States and Canada. It also became popular as a sales tool through promotions and advertising. Dealers and division personnel also wanted to take a tour.

"They had built some new buildings at the Proving Ground. In one building, they had a dining room that would seat over 500 people and an auditorium with 520 upholstered chairs. It had a revolving stage platform with the latest in lighting to highlight new models. There was also a large display area to show up to 40 cars. They even had a fleet of six chauffeured buses to shuttle VIPs on tours around the Proving Ground. These facilities would be used for a variety of business meetings including announcing new models for dealers.

"It was also possible to invite a friend or relative for a visit with preapproval. Such guests usually stayed for a clubhouse lunch and were then treated to a driving tour around the facility. It was great fun to take a young guy and tuck him into the back seat of a service car, then head for the North-South Straightaway to really stretch the car's legs. At each end of this high-speed multi-lane track were banked turnabouts. If you entered at the posted speed for your lane, the car would circumnavigate "hands off" reentering the straight track in the opposite direction. The favorite gag was to take a 120 mph run in the high-speed lane. Just as the car entered the turnabout, the driver would turn around, without taking his foot off the gas but remove his hands from the steering wheel, face the visitor in the rear seat, put a cigarette in his mouth, and ask for a light.

"I entertained and educated dignitaries, heads of state, kings, princes, oh yes, and all the automotive people too, from all over the world, about this showplace that everyone wanted to visit. During this time, I became acquainted with the top brass and familiar with all phases of General Motors. I presented lectures and gave tours of the General Motors Proving Ground for the next several years."

The stock market crash, October 29, 1929, known as Black Friday, took its toll on many jobs at General Motors. The Sales Activity was considered non-essential, and the program was discontinued.

"Every one of us attached to that department," Carl recalls, "got a 'pink slip'. We had 60 days to find another job. That was a real blow to me.

"I had made many acquaintances in the GM building, and one day when I was in Detroit, I stopped by the Chevrolet offices and ran into W. G. 'Spin' Llewellyn. He told me that Chevrolet was looking to hire a few service representatives for a special program. I interviewed and got the job. I worked out of the Houston Zone the next year, calling on dealers and promoting a General Motors program to modernize their service department.

My boss in Houston was Jim Marks, the Chevrolet Zone Service Manager.

One morning when I was at a dealership in Lufkin, Texas, Mr. Marks called me and said: "I just received a wire from your brother and thought I had better let you know."

Well, things started rushing through my head: did someone die?

Mr. Marks then asked if I would like him to read it to me over the phone.

I said," Yes, please."

The wire read: "Would you be interested in succeeding Mr. Newman at the Proving Ground? Signed D. P. Brother"

I started to laugh, which didn't go over well with Mr. Marks.

I said I think you'll see the initials D. P. before Brother.

Marks thought I had a brother at General Motors and was pulling some strings. Actually, he was my old boss at the Proving Ground.

At the time, I had mixed emotions about taking the job. I was still upset about being fired only a year earlier but I knew that if I didn't, it might jeopardize any advancements in the corporation. I drove back to Detroit, met with Mr. Brother, and accepted the job. As it turned out, that was the best decision I made during my time at General Motors."

My father was in his late 20s when he took control of the new Sales Activity. His bosses had enough confidence in him that they gave him considerably more responsibilities than his age would dictate. The year was 1931.

"The Sales Activity section grew like crazy", Carl said. "Twice as large as it was before. Before I was 30, I had 57 people working under me. I was there for roughly three years.

"When things slowed down, usually in January, they would assign me to some special activities away from the Proving Ground. They varied quite a bit.

"My boss in Detroit would call me in and say that one of the Zone offices, say California, was getting complaints about a technical issue and would send me for a week to collect first-hand information and bring it back to the division for correction.

"Another very interesting assignment was when I would relieve a manager at the General Motors permanent exhibit on the Steel Pier in Atlantic City, N.J. I did this on a few occasions and that's when I got my first taste of show business."

61 Auto Shows

The country was still in the depths of the Great Depression and that's when GM came up with a plan to put on a gigantic auto show to instill optimism and confidence in the future for the American public. R. H. Grant, V.P. Sales, came up with the idea of putting on a series of automobile shows in 61 communities throughout the United States in the spring of 1932. They would average 40 vehicles displayed for 9 days, all running simultaneously.

My father, along with several others, worked on preparing for this massive program for over five months. He was selected to be the manager of the Southwest Region and coordinate the show in several major cities. The Argonaut Realty Division of General Motors had leased a variety of properties for these week-long shows. Carl took three trips to each of his assigned cities. The first one was to set up local committees from the zone office personnel. Then follow-up trips to make sure there wouldn't be any problems and see that the shows would go off as planned.

Carl recalls: "On one trip to Oklahoma City, two young men, about my age, called one day and told me that they were in the movie industry and would like to rent me some portable searchlights to draw attention to the show. They even took me to their home to see the large lights, but my boss said it wasn't in the budget and turned them down. It wasn't until several years later that I discovered one of the young men that I had spent the afternoon with, had moved to California and made it big in the movie industry. His name was Howard Hughes."

"This was the era of the Big Bands. GM enlisted MCA (Music Corporation of America) to hire a named band to perform at each one of these shows. The band that was selected for Tulsa, Oklahoma, was not well known. The local dealers insisted on using a very popular band that was drawing large crowds. Even though it wasn't my decision, they took me to a local dance hall to see them. That's when I met Phil Harris and his brother. In the end, MCA was convinced to hire the Harris Brothers Band for the show."

In Dallas, Argonaut Realty had leased the Adolphus Hotel for the show. When my father arrived, he discovered that they didn't have an elevator to transport the cars to the mezzanine where the show was to be held. They thought they could get the 39 cars up there on skids through a narrow staircase with a block and tackle. This was unacceptable so after contacting Detroit, they moved the show to the Dallas Fairgrounds.

At each of these shows, General Motors would give away a new car. Attendees would fill out a registration card and put the stub in a box as they entered.

"I returned to Dallas about the third day of the show and met with my committee. They were experiencing larger-than-expected crowds at the fairgrounds. Then the GMC Truck Zone Manager, Mr. McDonald who was the committee chairman, asked how we were going to mix up all these entries.

"I said, "It's right there in your manual. Just get a carpenter to build a large round chicken-wire cage and turn them in that."

"McDonald then said: "Have you seen how many entries we have?"

"After a little discussion, Mr. McDonald came up with a solution. He had just sold a large fleet of cement trucks to a local contractor; I think around 12 and knew that they all hadn't been put in service yet. He called the contractor and got a brand-new cement mixer truck to use at the fairground.

"There was a huge crowd at the fairground the night of the show because you had to be present to win. Hundreds of boxes of entries were dumped into the mixer. It turned around several times, and then the mayor stuck his head in and pulled out the winning ticket.

"Needless to say, these shows were a tremendous success. It was a masterstroke. There were editorials in hundreds of newspapers with rave reviews. Some even gave General Motors credit for helping to turn the country around and help pull it out from the great depression."

The Waldorf-Astoria Show

"A year before the 61 cities shows, in 1931, Alfred P. Sloan, President of General Motors made arrangements with Lucius Boomer, General Manager of the Waldorf-Astoria Hotel, to hold an auto show in the world's leading hotel in the heart of New York City.

"Naysayers said it couldn't be done and no one would come. They couldn't have been more wrong. The show was held in January and ran for 9 days. It was a huge success and continued to be held there for the next 30 years."

My father recalls the following: "Gardner Cobb, with the General Motors Sales Activity Department, was in charge of the show and I was his assistant. A 29-year-old farm boy from Ohio, and the first time I had been to New York City. This was one of the most impressive things I ever did during my time at General Motors.

"The show was to be held in the huge Grand Ballroom on the 3rd floor. A room that could hold 3,500 people. All the preliminary arrangements had been made in Detroit and we had to execute them. We had to time everything down to the split-second. We were displaying 57 cars on the third floor and as I recall, it took a minute and thirty-six seconds per car in the elevator. You do the math. We had to get a special permit to park and bring the cars in from Park Avenue and Lexington Avenue. We even set up a temporary office in the second floor kitchen and had the telephone company set up a separate switchboard with two operators, just for the show.

"We had also arranged for 100 salesmen from local dealerships to work the show on two 50-man shifts. Each day the show would open at 9:00 a.m. and run till 11:00 p.m. Six nationally known orchestras held their hour-long radio broadcast from the show which brought in a lot of people. General Motors also hired 12 ushers. All the salesmen and ushers were fitted with a proper uniform.

"The day before the show opened to the general public, we were to hold an evening VIP reception for special dignitaries. We were all set and scheduled to bring the cars in at 2 o'clock but there was a luncheon in the Grand Ballroom and the guest speaker was Eleanor Roosevelt. She talked till almost 4 o'clock! We were all upset, but what could you do? She was the president's wife. We did get everything in place and finally were able to open the reception about an hour late.

"Oscar Tschirky, better known as Oscar of the Waldorf, was our direct contact and coordinated the event. I knew Oscar very well. He was a charming man. Toward the end of that first night's reception, I was standing with Oscar and Gardner Cobb, hoping everyone would leave so we could clean up.

"Gardner asked Oscar if he thought that the show was a success.

"Oscar, replying in his thick European accent, said, "I think so. You don't know these people, but I have to deal with them all the time. Over there is Mrs. Van Rensselaer, sitting on a running board and eating a cold chicken sandwich. Tomorrow, she will probably be complaining about the temperature of the Pheasant-under-glass that we served her.

"20,000 to 30,000 people a day visited the General Motors Motorama show. It was such a success that GM decided to put on a similar show at the Stevens (Conrad Hilton) Hotel in Chicago the next year. I worked at both the New York and Chicago shows for the next three years. They were some of my most memorable experiences at General Motors."

*1933 Waldorf Show — Grand Ballroom with
a Cadillac V-12 convertible display*

W.G. Holler

"In March of 1933, a new independent front suspension, patterned after the French Dubonnet system, was demonstrated to the heads of all five GM car brands. It dramatically improved the ride of the automobile. When asked if they should use this new suspension, GM's technology guru, Charles F. "Boss" Kettering proclaimed, "We can't afford not to do it." The feature was adopted across the board by Chevrolet, Pontiac, Oldsmobile, Buick, and Cadillac for the 1934 model year and marketed under the colorful name — Knee Action.

"The Proving Ground hosted thousands of Chevrolet dealers from all over the country, in the fall of 1933, to introduce and educate them about the revolutionary knee-action independent front suspension that would be standard on the 1934 models. The meetings were set up by regions with the regional manager in charge.

One manager stood out above everyone else. W.G. Holler was the Buffalo, N.Y. Regional Manager with about seven zones.

"After his second meeting, all of us at the Proving Ground realized what a dynamic man this Mr. Holler was." Long before motivational speakers became fashionable, Bill Holler was an institution! Automotive News described him as a spellbinder, a table-pounder, and an evangelist.

"Now, just before he was about to go on and address four hundred dealers for his last meeting, I heard the phone ring in my office, adjacent to the backstage.

"When I answered the phone, the operator said, "New York is calling Mr. Holler, is he there?"

I said, "Yes, he is but he's about to go on stage."

She said, "Just a minute please."

"When she came back, she said, "Mr. Sloan's office is calling Mr. Holler, can you get me Mr. Holler."

"Well now, that's something different! Mr. Sloan is the President of General Motors. I go and tell Mr. Holler that Mr. Sloan is on the line, and without any hesitation, he goes to my office and picks up the phone.

"I followed him in, just the two of us, and I heard him say, "Yes, Mr. Sloan, Yes sir, Thank you, Mr. Sloan", and when he finished, he turned to me and said, "You know what Carl? They just made me General Sales Manager of Chevrolet."

Now, the real punchline, that I'll never forget, is when he said,

"You know what, if I just say, Yes, No, Yes, No, at least I'll be 50 percent right."

Bill Holler said he would take the job for ten years during which time he set many sales records for Chevrolet that have never been matched. He established sales and training programs including Chevrolet's Quality Dealer Program and the Chevrolet School of Merchandising and Management. He also wrote a best-selling motivational sales book called 'Step Out and Sell' and founded the General Motors Dealers' Son School. His service to Chevrolet ended when he retired in 1945. He retired early and spent the rest of his time in Florida where his two sons were automobile dealers.

The Momma Story

In 1933, my father was living at the clubhouse with about ten other young single engineers with very little to do on the weekends. One Saturday someone said the American Legion was putting on a dance, so he and three friends hopped in a car and went into Milford, 4 miles away.

"We stood around for a while checking things out. We knew most of the available girls in the area and then we spotted a stranger. A little brunette sitting with Mr. and Mrs. Boyles. We all knew the Boyles quite well. He was the local postmaster.

"Curious, we asked around if anyone knew who she was.

"Someone said, "Don't you know? The American Legion is going to put on a play here and she just came in this afternoon.

She's going to be the coach, the director. Her name is Eleanor Smoot and she's from Anniston, Alabama."

"She started paying a lot of attention to me and I'm sure it was not because of my good looks. I think she had found out about my job, possibly from the Boyles, and that I had control of show equipment and personnel at the Proving Ground that might be able to help her with the play.

"As the night went on, we got together. She was cute as a button and had the most distinctive Southern accent I had ever heard. I also learned that she had been traveling for the last six years, working for the Wayne P. Sewell Company putting on hometown plays.

"This was a musical with local talent and would be held in the high school auditorium at Milford and just as she had figured out, I furnished spots, stage lights, and various drops for the play. She only arrived with a script and a trunk full of costumes and would have to arrange for everything else locally. It wound up that I was sending truckloads of stage equipment down to the high school auditorium and using our people to set it up. I had a lot of leeway and approval from my bosses. GM always wanted to support local community activities. Several Proving Ground personnel even tried out and got parts in the musical. She even talked me into being the leading man, even though I can't carry a tune in a bucket.

"We would go on a drive, stop and she would coach me on how to sing these songs. I'll never forget the trouble I had with this one song "When You Waltz With The One You Love." As it turned out, I made it through, and the play was a huge success.

"During the two and a half weeks we spent together, we seemed to get along beautifully. I was so happy that she accepted me. I fell for her like a ton of bricks. She was just what I was looking for.

"Before she left, she told me that she was getting very tired of traveling and we agreed to stay in contact with each other. We started writing letters several times a week. I made a commitment that I would meet her in Alabama when I got my vacation. And I did just that!

"I didn't have a personal car. Everything I was doing, up to that time, was work-related and I had access to a variety of cars at the Proving Ground. It ended up that I bought a 1934 Chevrolet convertible with what we would call today, all the bells and whistles, from Harry Klingler, General Sales Manager for Chevrolet. This is the car I drove to Alabama. I really wanted to 'put on the dog' with this convertible.

"I took my vacation in August of 1933 and drove my new Chevrolet convertible to Anniston, Alabama. I met her mother, Emma, for the first time. Her father, Jacob, had passed away when Eleanor was just two years old.

"During our correspondence, we had made plans to visit her sister, Florine, in Tampa, Florida. Well, her mother had a dim view of her daughter going on a long trip with this slick man from General Motors, so we had to make the entire trip in one day. We got to Florine's at dark and spent the next few days going to the beach and getting acquainted. Then it was time to go back to Anniston and we had to make it in one day.

"I drove back to Detroit and immediately started figuring

out how I could get back to Alabama. We were preparing for the Waldorf auto show coming up in the first part of January. I went to my boss and asked if I could get off a few days before the show. He approved and I made a trip from Detroit to New York City by way of Atlanta, Georgia. I took the train to Atlanta, where we had an assembly plant, and made arrangements to get a company car for the weekend.

"It was at this time that we got engaged. I asked and she said yes. I was on cloud nine. We set the date. One we wouldn't forget. We were married at her mother's home in Anniston, Alabama on February 22, 1934 (Washington's Birthday)."

My mother passed away on October 7, 1989, from complications of Alzheimer's disease. She outlived my father by seven years. They had been married for 48 years.

Oldsmobile Division

After they were married, my father decided that he wanted to leave the Proving Ground and get into the field with one of the car divisions. He was interviewed and was hired by Oldsmobile. His first assignment was with the Buffalo, NY Zone. He and his new wife moved to Jamestown, NY where he would call on dealers in that area as their District Sales Representative.

"My Zone Manager, Clem DeBarry, had a great deal of influence on me as my first boss in the field. Each month, the District Representatives were called in to review what they had accomplished with their dealers. Our primary responsibility was to sell them vehicles and other GM programs. We also assisted them by pointing out areas in their operation that needed improvement. Two major problems for many dealers were excessive used car inventories and accounts receivable. We were ranked on almost everything our dealers did. I took my job seriously and worked very hard, and as a result, exceeded almost every goal they had set for me. DeBarry made me go above and beyond what I thought my capabilities were. He was a driver, very strict but fair. I carry many of his principles with me today."

The time my father spent calling on dealers established his confidence that he could run a successful automobile dealership. His years in the field with Oldsmobile were a better education than a college degree. He understood all the problems to avoid and embraced the things that the successful dealers were doing right. It all started with his first boss and mentor, Clem DeBarry, and culminated in Cheyenne with Halladay Motors.

My father's job kept him away from home during the week. They had only been married about three weeks and my mother was looking for something to keep her busy. This is when she got involved with the local community theater group. With all her acting and coaching experience, they welcomed her with open arms. She got the lead in one of their upcoming productions.

A few years later, while reading a newspaper, my mother turned to my father, pointed to a photograph, and said: "That's the young girl that was in the play with me in Jamestown." Her name was Lucille Ball.

They lived in an apartment in Jamestown most of the time, but for two summers, during July, August, and September, they leased a delightful cabin on Chautauqua Lake. They made some good friends on the lake. My father even got an old boat that he was constantly fixing. It was one of the best memories of their early marriage. The cabin on the lake was the first real house they lived in, and it was during this time that my mom was pregnant with my sister, Barbara. She was born on September 11, 1935.

After three and a half years in Jamestown, the regional manager thought my father was ready to handle a larger district and transferred him to Wheeling, West Virginia. His dealers were located in three states along the Ohio River — Ohio, West Virginia, and Pennsylvania. In his recorded biography, he recalls many stories of the problems and successes of his time there. Here's one of the stories he loved to tell.

"We had several towns where we were not represented, and it was my job to find and sign up an Oldsmobile dealer. In one of our 'open points', Spencer, West Virginia, I found a filling station operator that met all the criteria. His initial investment was to purchase one vehicle, a large porcelain service sign, and the special tools required to service the cars.

"To ensure that every new dealer received the special tools, they were put in the trunk of the first car ordered. My new dealer picked up his new Oldsmobile at the warehouse in Pittsburgh. A few weeks later, when I contacted him, I found out that he had already sold his first car.

"He told me everything went fine except for one thing. "See here on the invoice, you billed me $37 for a tool kit and I had a heck of a time convincing my customer to take those tools with him."

I was born in Wheeling, West Virginia, on June 21, 1939, a few weeks before my father was transferred to the Pittsburgh Zone. I had some complications and the doctor insisted that I remain in the hospital for a while. My parents moved to a new home in Pittsburgh, Pennsylvania and after about six weeks, my father returned, picked me up, put me in a basket in the back seat of his car, (no child seat or seat belt), and took me to my new home. The only time I lived in Wheeling was when I was in the hospital, but it will always be on my passport.

This move was considered a promotion, and he assumed more responsibility. His new job was City Manager for Oldsmobile in metropolitan Pittsburgh. He was calling on 16 dealers that accounted for over half of the volume of the entire Zone. One advantage of this new position: he was rarely away from home overnight.

"Allegheny County Motor Co., my largest dealership, was selling over 1200 Oldsmobiles a year. Ed McKean was the dealer and an excellent businessman. Their many innovative programs kept them on top. A very successful one was the Used Car 'Try-A-Week' program. I probably learned more about the retail automobile business from Ed McKean and his associates than any other dealer in my lifetime.

"In 1940 there was a problem with used car clean-up. The 1941 model was going to have some big changes and there were way too many used cars in dealers' inventories. Oldsmobile put on a national contest for the 135 district managers in the US to reduce these inventories. My dealers came through for me and I won the top prize, a new 98 Oldsmobile Sedan. I didn't need another car, so I sold it to one of my dealers for $1,200.

"Oldsmobile's national market share was 5.5%. Later that year they came out with another contest for district managers. They paid incentives for 1/2%, 1%, and 1 1/2% improvement. I increased my market share to 7% and received a $1,000 bonus. I took the $1,000 bonus and the $1,200 from the sale of the car and purchased GM stock."

Four years later, this money would help with the establishment of the new dealership in Cheyenne.

A tragic accident happened to my father while living in Pittsburgh. It was April 19, 1941. He was working on a project, at home, in his basement, when a piece of metal from a grinding wheel entered his left eye. He spent 19 days in the hospital, but they could not save his sight. With a very good prosthetic and the fact that he wore glasses, very few people knew that he only had one eye. It didn't affect his ability to function in any way. I wasn't even aware of the accident till many years later. He rarely talked about it. In my research, I ran across a statement that he had saved. The total bill for his 19-day stay in the hospital was $127.50.

Oldsmobile and World War II

The day Pearl Harbor was attacked everything changed. All automobile production stopped, and all manufacturing plants were converted to build products in support of the war effort. My father was called back to Lansing, Michigan to be in charge of the Aircraft Armament Training School. Oldsmobile had already been making aircraft armament for lend-lease to our allies in Europe for about a year. Oldsmobile had agreed, along with the US Army's Aberdeen Proving Ground, to train 300 armorers a week.

"We were charged with setting up a school to train our troops on how to use these weapons. Starting a school from scratch was not an easy task. This required finding housing, building class-rooms, and hiring civilian instructors. My team and I accomplished all of this in about three weeks."

Over the next year and a half, my father, his staff, and 57 instructors trained over 18,000 soldiers from both Army and Navy branches of the service on the guns Oldsmobile was building. The training covered .50 caliber, 20mm, and 37mm aircraft-mounted machine guns. They also provided training for the 75mm semi-automatic artillery cannon that was mounted on the B-25 bomber. Toward the end of the war, the US Army Air Force took over all armament training.

A colonel in the fifth ordinance district, Philadelphia, conceived an idea to put on a show for the general public to promote the sale of war bonds. They would invite all manufacturers who produced products for the war effort to put on a display. The huge John Wanamaker department store in Philadelphia dedicated its entire eleventh floor for this promotion.

"The school was closing so three other instructors, and I were given the job to set up a booth to show how we trained the armorers. The final test, to see if the student had learned all he could about the weapon, was a blindfold test. We used the 20mm M2 gun and set up the bench and display like it would look in the classroom. As I recall, there were 213 individual parts. It took the average student forty minutes to assemble and disassemble the gun but during the demonstrations, my instructors and I got the time down to less than thirteen minutes. We would do this presentation and blindfold test every half hour from 10:00 am when they opened to 9:00 pm. I was there for six weeks till I got a call from Lansing. They wanted me back in the field."

Gun School demonstration — Carl
Sr. on the left in a shop coat

Omaha

During the war, Oldsmobile had closed five zone offices and attached those dealers to an adjacent zone. "They wanted me to take charge of the Omaha territory, but I would report to the Kansas City zone office.

"I called mom and said, 'We're moving to Omaha.'"

"I knew it would be difficult to find a place to stay in Omaha, but I got lucky. A friend of mine at Oldsmobile had a brother who was a Realtor there. I took the train to Omaha and met with Mr.

Quinn. After I explained my situation, he told me there might be a rental available if the owner would agree to it.

"Joseph A. Suneg, a Catholic priest, had a beautiful home in downtown Omaha. He was in the process of building the landmark St. Margaret Mary Church. The parish had purchased him a home close to the new church, and he was willing to rent his home to the right person. My father met Father Suneg at the church site that day and he must have been the right person. Our family moved into Father Suneg's home about a month later.

"There were 220 dealers in the old Omaha Zone. It covered all of Nebraska except the panhandle, the southern tier of South Dakota, and about two-thirds of Iowa. I learned that in the last full year of production, they sold a total of 2,700 cars. By comparison, in my last job in Pittsburgh, I had 16 dealers, all within 20 miles and they sold 5,800 cars. Here I was again, traveling hundreds of miles, mostly putting out fires. For a year and a half, I was constantly trying to keep customers happy and dealers in business.

"I was in Yankton, South Dakota helping a new dealer, after dinner, set up his parts department when I got a call and my god, it was Mom. She was hysterical! She was crying and said there was something terribly wrong with Carl Jr. and the doctor was on his way. Well, I dropped everything and drove back to Omaha as fast as I could, ignoring the 35 mph speed limit in effect at that time. I went straight to the hospital and for the next thirty-six hours, it was nip and tuck whether he would survive. The diagnosis was Pneumococcal Meningitis."

Needless to say, I survived. I'm still alive and kickin' at 85 years old.

My father, Carl Halladay Sr., moved himself and his family; his wife Eleanor, Barbara (9), and Carl Jr. (5) from Omaha, Nebraska to Cheyenne, Wyoming in October 1944. He had spent 20 years with General Motors… Oh, Wait! That's the beginning of Chapter 1.

Years of smoking finally caught up with my father. Carl R. Halladay Sr passed away at 78 on June 3, 1982, from complications of emphysema.

Carl Sr.'s Hobbies and Other Interests

My father was a tinkerer. He could fix almost anything. His curiosity led him to get involved with all the latest gadgets, probably because of his engineering background.

Photography and woodworking were two of his early hobbies. I remember he had one of the very first ShopSmiths, a woodworking bench that could be converted into a table saw, drill press, wood lathe, sander, and many other tools. I remember spending many hours in our basement learning lots of skills from him and I continue to use them in the many projects I do to this day.

His photography started early with a simple box camera and progressed through all phases ending up with an SLR and a full bag of lenses and attachments. I also remember a twin-lens Rolex.

He built a darkroom in the basement of his 8th Ave home, complete with an enlarger, chemical trays, running water, drying racks, and everything you would need to develop black-and-white photos. He never got into printing photos in color.

Home movies were also a major hobby. It started when my

sister, Barbara, was born in 1935. I still have his hand-wound Bell & Howell Filmo 8mm movie camera. I'm glad he took so many home movies. I'm having them digitized now.

The Cabin

In 1949 my father purchased a cabin on 100 acres about 35 miles west of Cheyenne, off Harriman Road. This was his favorite weekend retreat. Being raised on a farm it took him back to his roots where he could mow the pasture, fix the fence, repair the barn, or just relax from a busy work week. He even opened a spring and built a small fishpond in the pasture above the cabin. We all had fun feeding and catching the stocked trout.

Every year in late August he would hold a company picnic for all the employees and their families. The sales department and service department would go head to head in a softball game. Children took part in sack races, watermelon eating contests, and a variety of other games. We brought several rolls of quarters and made sure each child got one or two for their prizes. A fun husband and wife game that always got a laugh was the raw egg tossing contest where you stepped back a pace after each toss. We had a couple of kegs of beer and soft drinks for the kids, and the food was usually catered. We ordered in advance for 100-plus people and brought it to the cabin in aluminum trays. We ate a lot of Kentucky Fried Chicken over the years.

As I was growing up, we spent almost every weekend at the cabin. In the beginning, we had two horses that our rancher neighbor, Foss Lawson, looked after during the week. I learned to drive at the cabin in a 1939 Ford Model A pickup that we kept to haul trash. I built a small log cabin when I was around 12 years old. We were never at a lack for something to do.

Barbara

My sister, Barbara, married Phil Yarter in 1957. They met while Barbara was attending Northwestern University and Phil was working in the area. Phil was from Cheyenne, but they had never met there. His parents, Ed, and Elsi Yarter owned and operated the Trail Cafe. After they were married, they settled in Denver and had four girls: Jennifer, Carole, Amy, and Nanci. Even though Barbara was never involved in the car business, she and her family were always included in all the dealership's social events.

For many years while the kids were growing up our two families would get together for Thanksgiving at their home in Denver and then they would come to our home in Cheyenne for the Halladay Motors Christmas party. On several occasions, Phil would play Santa. This was a special time for all the cousins to have together.

In the summer, the Yarter family spent several weekends at the cabin with my parents and of course came to the company picnic. When my parents both passed away, Barbara received the cabin in their will. Her daughter Carole is taking care of it now.

The Christmas Party

The Halladay Motors company Christmas Party was by far the biggest and most remembered dealership family event of the year. I still have employees' children come up to me today and recall how special that event was to them.

From the very beginning, my father believed strongly that the employees' families should be recognized for the very important part they played as part of the Halladay Motors team. The annual Christmas party started from the very beginning. In 1944, only two months after opening the filling station at 3920 Central Ave., all five employees met for a brief time in the office, and each received a not-so-large turkey. The next year was better and by this time ten employees and their families all received presents at a real Christmas party. This started a tradition that has continued today.

Every year my father would make a list of all the employees' children. In some years there would be over 120 children. Two families, I recall had six children each, Buzz Bartels and Dick Adams.

Cheyenne didn't have a 'big box' toy store at that time so he would make a trip to a warehouse in Denver where he could get 12-15 of the latest toys for one age group.

After the shopping was done, all the presents ended up in our basement and he personally wrapped and labeled, with individual names, every toy. There were always a couple of extra presents in case of a recently hired employee or a mistake had been made. Later I helped with the buying and wrapping. Of course, Santa was always the one to hand out the presents at the party.

Throughout the first three decades, Christmas parties were held in the dealership showroom. Then sometime in the mid-70s, we began to hold them at the Cheyenne Country Club. We would have a traditional Christmas turkey dinner with all the trimmings, occasionally some entertainment, and of course, Santa handing out presents.

How this all started is best described in Carl Sr's own words taken from one of our Rocket Roundup newsletters from 1962:

"I am reminded at the moment of how our annual Christmas party for our employees and their children came into being. Back in 1925, when I first began working for General Motors, my job assignment was that of Test Technician at the General Motors Proving Ground… located out in the country forty miles from Detroit. It was four miles to the nearest village of Milford, Michigan.

The Proving Ground was quite new then, having opened only the year before. There were only about two hundred employees there then, most of them married and with families. They lived in nearby villages and on small farms in the vicinity.

Mr. Alfred P. Sloan was President of General Motors then and he didn't forget us at this outpost of General Motors. Prior to each Christmas, Mr. Sloan would send his personal check for a sizable sum to the Director of the Proving Grounds, together with his request to have a Christmas party for the employees and their families. Those of us who lived at the Grounds (I was single at the time) had the pleasant task of buying gifts and wrapping them for everyone.

After eight years at the Proving Ground, I resolved that if I were ever fortunate enough to have my own family of employees, I would perpetuate Mr. Sloan's idea within my own organization. And that's how our annual Christmas party at Halladay Motors was brought into being."

*1949 Christmas party in the showroom
at 408 E. Lincolnway*

Carl R. Halladay, Jr.

Junior

Yes, I am a 'Junior'. Carl Raymond Halladay Junior. That moniker, 'junior', when used alone, always stuck in my wife's craw. "A forty-year-old man and you still call him Junior." She was born and raised in southern Oregon where it may have had more of a 'redneck' meaning.

My mother, on the other hand, who named me, was from the deep south, Anniston, Alabama. To carry on the tradition, not only the surname but also the first name was looked on with pride and prominence in the community. When our son was born, my mother suggested that we name him Carl III and call him Trey. Joanne would have no part of that, and we ended up naming him Scott.

We had two daughters and Scott, who is handicapped and has never been married. Our branch of the Halladay tree will end when Scott and I are gone.

Carl Jr.

Growing up as the son of a prominent business figure isn't easy. You grow up in their shadow and there are always expectations that you will carry on in their footsteps, especially in the car business. I have known many second, third, and even fourth-generation dealers' sons and daughters throughout the state and nation. Here in Cheyenne, Brian Tyrrell is a third-generation car dealer, and John Dinneen, before he sold his dealership, was a fourth-generation dealer.

In my later years, I have become more accepting of my name and the role I played in the success of our dealership. I have always been proud of the fact that I was Carl Sr.'s son. When we were working together, I always signed my name simply 'Carl Jr.' and still do today.

Early History

I was five years old when we moved to Cheyenne. I remember very little before that except what I learned through photos, home movies, and family stories.

We rented a house about two blocks from 19th St. and Logan Ave on Cheyenne Place. It was literally on the edge of town. I remember our block was full, with 3 or 4 houses on the next block and then open fields till you reached the V.A. Center. I entered kindergarten at Alta Vista Elementary School in the fall of 1944. Oddly enough, my future wife, Joanne, would teach second grade there for several years in the 80s and 90s.

The following year we moved to the Avenues which was much closer to the business. Our first house was 422 W. 1st Ave. Then after a couple of years, we moved to 415 W. 3rd Avenue. This was the house I grew up in and lived there till I went to college.

In 1945 I spent the first half of my first grade attending Churchill School while the brand-new Deming Elementary School was being built. I finished at Deming and then I went to McCormick Junior High School, downtown, and like everyone else, we walked every day, rain, snow, or shine.

In 1954 my parents convinced me that a private military high school would provide me with an excellent educational opportunity. My father had a great respect for military discipline and now that he could afford to send me, he thought that I would benefit from the experience.

I spent the next three years at New Mexico Military Institute in Roswell, New Mexico. I graduated high school there in 1957. It was an experience I have never regretted.

After high school, I attended the University of Wyoming. At the end of my freshman year with my grades not being what they should have been, and the possibility of being drafted into the Army, I enlisted in the Navy for four years.

Joined the Navy 1958-1962

I had a very good experience in the Navy. My boot camp was in San Diego, California and when it came time to assign me a job, I got lucky. They recommended I become a Communications Technician. So, I did.

At the time I had no idea what it was but later found out that a CT was part of the security group of the Navy. Their job was to listen to and transcribe communications in several different languages from listening posts all over the world and send them back to the National Security Agency in Washington, D.C. to be analyzed. All of this was pre-computers as we know them today and cryptographic communications were mostly carried out with mechanical systems. I was part of the administrative end of the security group and went to Yeoman school in Bainbridge, Maryland for my training.

My first duty was at a Naval Air Station in Port Layaute, Morocco, North Africa where I spent a year and a half. We had 3 large military bases in Morocco at that time. Two Air Force bases and the Naval Air Station, where I spent the first half of my overseas duty.

The second half was spent at a small Radio Communication Station about 10 miles out of town. The Naval Air Station was located about 160 miles south of the Straights of Gibraltar on the Atlantic coast. The weather was beautiful for the most part with one exception. The winds would change direction during a sirocco, and instead of coming off the ocean, they would come directly from the Sahara desert. The temperatures would go through the roof. I remember that for several days, that summer, the temperature remained above 120 degrees.

The last two years of my enlistment were spent at the Cheltenham Naval Communication Station outside of Washington, D.C., close to Andrews Air Force Base. Although I was part of the security group and had a top-secret clearance, I never knew any secrets. I spent four years in the Navy, and I was never aboard a ship. I was honorably discharged on August 3, 1962, as a Second Class Petty Officer CT2.

Had I not had my father's business to return to, I may have reenlisted in the Navy. I would have immediately been promoted to first-class petty officer and had my choice of duty stations. Japan and the Far East were considered choice duty at that time. I often think back and consider "what might have been" because on January 23, 1968, five and a half years after I was discharged, the USS Pueblo was captured, and 82 crew members were held prisoner and tortured by the North Koreans for 11 months. The USS Pueblo was a 'listening ship' and was one of a select few boats I could have been assigned to.

After leaving the Navy, I returned to the University of Wyoming for the fall semester of 1962. I had pledged to the Sigma Chi fraternity and became active when I returned. Being at least four years older than any of my sophomore classmates, and being over the age of 21, my social life took an entirely different direction. Most of my friends were upperclassmen or graduate students.

My first week back, I remember very distinctly walking into the Brown and Gold coffee shop, across from the campus, and seeing a blond-haired kid whaling away on a nylon string guitar. Of course, I had to introduce myself. His name was Bent John Pouttu. We became close friends and played together for the next two years. 1962, the folk music era was in full swing. It was during this time that I learned every song by Bob Dylan, Joan Baez, Harry Belafonte, The Kingston Trio, and almost every other folk song from that era. We were constantly trying out new instruments and swapping with each other. I still have John Pouttu's Goya G-20 guitar.

John Pouttu also introduced me to some of his friends. Ray Jaquot and Keith Hull were part of the Outing Club and when they weren't listening to folk music they were talking about mountaineering. They had all attended Casper College where they learned their rock climbing skills under Walt Bailey, who had formed the Casper College Outing Club. When they transferred to Laramie, they formed the University of Wyoming Outing Club.

That summer, Ray assembled a group of seven of us to travel to Jackson Hole and climb the Grand Teton. The following year, eight of us embarked on a nine-day wilderness hike from Dubois to Cody, Wyoming. When I was playing music, I thought that I would never get involved in long hikes or mountain climbing but when I did, it was some of my best memories of those years at the University. I completed two years at UW before joining my father at the dealership in the summer of 1964.

Joanne Hansen — My wife for 52 years

Joanne Hansen grew up in Grants Pass, Oregon, the 5th of 6 children. After high school, she enrolled at Oregon State University in Corvallis, Oregon. Obtaining some college loans and working at the university library, she put herself through school and graduated with a degree in elementary education in 1964. She loved to tell this next story on how she got to Cheyenne.

"Just after graduating, my class was having a big beer party (I didn't drink) and everyone was asking each other where they were going to apply for a teaching job. As a joke someone put up a map of the Western U.S. on the wall and

we all threw darts at it. Mine landed in Wyoming. All I knew about Wyoming was Yellowstone National Park and Cheyenne.

My older sister, Marie, also a teacher, had attended a summer course at the University of Colorado in Boulder so I thought I would ask her about Cheyenne. She said 'Oh, you don't want to go there; it's hot and windy'. She had taken one trip to Cheyenne to see a Cheyenne Frontier Days rodeo. I thought to myself 'My older sister has been telling me what to do all my life, well I'll just show her' and I wrote to the Department of Education in Cheyenne, and they sent me a contract in the mail. I signed it and headed to Cheyenne."

Joanne didn't have a driver's license and had never driven a car. She arrived in Cheyenne in August 1964 on the Union Pacific Railroad and had made arrangements to stay with a friend's family for the first few days. She was so naive that she thought she could find a nice apartment complex with a swimming pool and close enough to her school that she could walk.

In 1964, Boeing was in the middle of its missile modification program, and every apartment in Cheyenne was taken. To make matters worse, she was assigned to a brand new school on the outskirts of town, Jessup. She finally met two other new teachers with the same dilemma, Rosella Stralow, and Bev Thompson. The three of them shared a basement apartment in a private home a block north of Hoy's Drugstore. Her new roommates drove her to school until she could get her own transportation.

The family she had stayed with when she first arrived in Cheyenne, had a son who had a friend who was a salesman at Halladay Motors and set us up on a double date.

Joanne always said that her dream car would be a Mustang Convertible. Well, I didn't sell Fords, so she ended up with a 1964 Cutlass Supreme Coupe, blue with a white interior. Since I was brand new to the sales force, our top salesman, Lee Tafoya, helped me out with the sale. He told her she didn't have to have any money down (since she didn't have any) and there would just be a big balloon payment at the end. Now, I'm not sure it's true but after we were married Joanne swore that every time I wrote a check for the payment, I would say: "I wish we had given you a better deal."

At the time I was also sharing a basement apartment with Bill Bagley. We were Sigma Chi fraternity brothers at the University of Wyoming, and we both ended up back in Cheyenne, in the summer of 1964. Bill was running Teno Roncalio's campaign for the US Congress and would eventually move to Washington D.C. with him when Teno won. That's where he met his wife Margi. When he and Margi returned to Cheyenne, Bill joined a law firm and the four of us would become close friends.

Joanne and I were engaged within three months of our first date and started planning a wedding for the next summer. After the initial shock, my mother began making arrangements. The wedding list was looking more like the Country Club directory than the simple wedding we had planned. Joanne didn't have any family in Cheyenne, and she finally made an ultimatum: "If you want to marry me, we're going to elope." So, we did.

We were married on June 12, 1965, at the Methodist Church in Fort Collins, Colorado. It happened so fast that Bill Bagley, who was going to be my best man, was out of town and so I had one of the lawyers from his firm, Ward White stand in as best man and Rosella Stralow was Joanne's maid of honor.

Our Children

Returning to Cheyenne after our honeymoon camping in the Grand Tetons, we settled down in Western Hills. Our first home was on Golden Hills and five years later we moved to a larger home a few blocks away on Custer Street. Our three children grew up there. They all went to Jessup Elementary School and then walked across the new pedestrian bridge to McCormick Jr. High School and Central High School.

Susie, our oldest, was born on February 8, 1967. While attending Arizona State University she took the second semester of her junior year to study abroad. She attended the University of London. She had only been there a few weeks when she met her future husband, Michael Hart. She stayed in London that summer and worked in an English pub. She returned to ASU and finished with a degree in Education. Susie and Michael were married in London and spent the next eight years working in England. They returned to the States in 1996 and had two children, Emily, and Ethan. They currently live in Omaha, Nebraska.

A little over a year later Scott was born on April 20, 1968. At age 8, when he was in second grade, he had his first seizure. In the many years after that, we had him examined, tested, and seen by specialists throughout the country. Finally, in 1985, we spent a month in Canada at the Montreal Neurological Institute where he was diagnosed with a form of epilepsy called Lennox Gastaut Syndrome. Medication helps but he still has seizures daily. He currently resides in Sheridan, Wyoming in a group home run by Rehabilitation Services of Northeast Wyoming, RENEW, now called Beacon Independency Center. He's been there since March 1989 and is doing fine.

Cindy was born on December 15, 1970. After graduating high school, she enrolled at the University of Wyoming. A year later she transferred to the University of Northern Arizona and enrolled in their design program. Little did she know that they would cancel the program the next year, so she transferred once again and finished her bachelor's degree at Colorado State University in Fort Collins. While working in Denver she met and married Brian Bahrenburg. They have two boys, Dylan and Logan, and live in Westminster, Colorado.

Family outing
Story, Wyoming

My mother passed away on October 7, 1989. Later that year Joanne and I moved into her home that she and my father built on 8th Avenue. It was one of the nicest locations in Cheyenne, right across from Lyons Park. A few years later, after I sold the business, we built a winter home in Goodyear, Arizona. We eventually moved to a townhome in North Cheyenne but were still maintaining two houses and had been traveling back and forth as snowbirds for 18 years. Then finally, in 2012 we decided to go down to one home and moved to Arizona permanently.

We were happily married for fifty-two years. Joanne passed away on November 27, 2017, on her 77th birthday.

Carl Jr.'s Hobbies and Other Interests

Music has always played an important part in my life. I got my first guitar in 1947 when I was 8 years old. It was a ¾-sized Harmony and I still have that guitar today. Not sure how it survived all those years but it's hanging on my wall and still playable thanks to my good friend and luthier, Bob Westbrook.

I played guitar all through grade school, high school, college, and the Navy. When I returned to Cheyenne in 1964, I met Don Williams. Don was a guitar and tenor banjo player. He was also learning to play the 5-string banjo. We immediately became friends and shared our passion for these string instruments. By this time, he was the owner and operator of Monks Auto Upholstery, a couple of blocks from the dealership. We would meet for coffee at the Coffee Cup Cafe several times a week.

Don was active in the Lyons Club at that time and was playing tenor banjo on their float in the Frontier Days Parades. He was also performing at the Old Fashion Melodrama. He got two other friends and me to form a group to play an 'olio' act at the melodrama. Rhea Sahler was directing the play that year. The characters' names were all based on Wyoming cities. For example, the lead was *Rocky Springs*, for the Wyoming town of Rock Springs. Rhea thought that it would be funny if there was a philharmonic string quartet in the tiny town (population 282) of Chugwater, Wyoming. She is credited for giving us the name of our band that has survived for over fifty years.

The Chugwater Philharmonic String Quartet

We all got together at Don's shop about a week before our first performance at the melodrama and put together a list of some basic folk songs that we all knew. Then we dressed up in some old clothes that looked more like Hobos than Hillbillies. Don played 5-string banjo, Stan Christensen, guitar, Wayne Land, bass, and I was playing mandolin. Don had a great sense of humor and told a lot of jokes. This quickly became part of our routine and in later years we used to say: "We were doing 'Hee Haw' five years before it was on TV."

The melodrama had two shows nightly so instead of staying backstage for an hour we went outside and played on the street for anyone who would listen. Sometimes we wandered over to the Plains Hotel bar to have a little liquid courage (as if we needed it) for the next performance. Those were fun days and they only got better.

Sam Blumenthal was the band teacher at Central High School and in 1971 he was approached by Larry Wise, the local representative for the H.D. Lee Company, to provide music for their Frontier Days activities. Lee Riders had a 'Big Pants' float with a clown walking alongside handing out stickers to the kids along the parade route. Sam had just started playing tenor guitar with our Chugwater group and thought this would be a perfect fit. This is when we donned the rodeo clown outfits. We performed for the H.D. Lee Company in all the parades and pancake breakfasts for the next 8 years until Wrangler replaced them as the official Professional Rodeo Cowboy Association's national sponsor.

Craig Lewis and Coors Beer then stepped up and sponsored us for the next eight years. We built the Coors float and used it as the stage when the pancake breakfast was held in the City Center parking lot. A few years later the breakfast was moved to the new Depot Plaza.

July 27, 1989, we were lined up and waiting for the parade to start when Scott Benning, with the Public Relations Committee, stopped by. He said that there were two New York models in town for a photo shoot and asked if one could ride on our float.

How could we refuse? We spent the next hour, before the parade started, with this attractive young lady. She was decked out in a spectacular gold, cowboy-styled, pants suit. None of us had any idea who she was but she sure looked good in that pants suit. Arthur Elgort, a nationally known fashion photographer, and his assistant chased us around the entire parade route taking several hundred photos. A full-page photo of me playing guitar and standing next to the model was published in the October 1989 issue of Italian Vogue Magazine.

When I got home that evening I told my daughter Susie about the New York model that I had spent the morning with and when I told her who it was, she screamed and had a fit. Her name was Cindy Crawford.

The Cheyenne Frontier Days Indian Committee was assigned to run the three free pancake breakfasts in partnership with the Cheyenne Kiwanis Club. This all-volunteer committee was responsible for coordinating the entertainment during the two-hour breakfasts, on Monday, Wednesday, and Friday mornings. Activities included arranging for the Native American dance performance, recognizing the General Committee and Royalty, introducing the Thunderbirds, and much more.

The Cheyenne Kiwanis Club did an amazing job of cooking up all those pancakes and serving them up with ham, butter, syrup, and coffee or milk. The line was already several blocks long when they started at 7 a.m. and on most days they served over 10,000 people in two hours. They sat on wooden benches and watched the entertainment while they ate their breakfast.

The Chugwater Philharmonic was the "house band" for these pancake breakfasts and I was personally involved in entertaining these audiences at every breakfast, for over 30 years.

After our band quit, Bob Mathews, our fiddler, took over and has been entertaining at the pancake breakfast with his family band, Country Club, ever since.

Seventeen people performed with our quartet. Yes, we were always a quartet, but we would add plus one, plus two, or sometimes even minus one. The final group of our 40-year plus consisted of: Bob Mathews-fiddle, Dennis Coelho-5 string banjo, Ron Poelma-bass, and Don Miller and me on guitar.

Chugwater Philharmonic String Quartet, plus one

Happy Jack Mountain Music Festival

January 1988, I got a call from Gloria Gapter. She was the Special Event Coordinator for the Wyoming State Parks and Cultural

Resources. She told me that she and the Park Superintendent for Curt Gowdy State Park, Pat Thompson, had been talking about putting on an event that would highlight the beautiful rock amphitheater at the park. She was familiar with the Chugwater Philharmonic and asked if I would be interested in working with the state parks to put on a bluegrass festival. Well, this was right up my alley. How could I refuse?

During the next several months, we planned the event, set up a 501(c)(3) "Friends of Curt Gowdy State Park," enlisted volunteers, hired the bands and held our first festival July 2-4, 1988. This turned out to be quite an undertaking. Curt Gowdy State Park is halfway between Cheyenne and Laramie on Happy Jack Road. Almost the entire infrastructure to put on the festival had to be hauled to the venue 23 miles from Cheyenne. You couldn't just run to a store if you forgot something.

Well-known bands from the area entertained every year. Among them were The Bluegrass Patriots from Fort Collins, CO, Turtle Creek from Nebraska, High Plains Tradition from Denver, and, of course, The Chugwater Philharmonic String Quartet from Cheyenne. In addition to the bands the first few years included a fiddle contest. After we were established, we attracted more regional and national bands to headline the festival. Some of the names, known well in the bluegrass community were: The Dusty Miller Bluegrass Band from Tennessee, Loose Ties from Jackson Hole, Pete Wernick's Live Five, Jim & Jesse and the Virginia Boys, The Special Consensus, Claire Lynch & The Front Porch String Band, Tim O'Brien & the O'Boys, and Lou Reid, Terry Baucom & Carolina.

In 1989, the Chugwater Philharmonic String Quartet was playing at a festival in Longmont, Colorado when I ran into Pete Kuykendall, publisher of the trade magazine, Bluegrass Unlimited. We had just finished our second festival and as I was showing him my scrapbook, he pointed at a very small photo and asked, "Could you send me a copy of that photo?" I sent him the photo and to my amazement, he used it for the cover of the January 1990 Festival Schedule issue. Pete and his wife Kitsy later accepted my invitation and attended our 1991 festival.

Finally, in 1995, we were informed that the State of Wyoming's budget constraints and changes in priorities did not include any more money for projects like a bluegrass festival. The State Parks had funded the festivals from the beginning and because we wanted to maintain affordable ticket prices, most years we just broke even. I was sad that it was over but frankly, I was running out of gas.

We had eight great years and I'm sure that many people still have fond memories of The Happy Jack Mountain Music Festival.

The Happy Jack Mountain Music Festival
on the cover of Bluegrass Unlimited

Bit-O-Wyo Horse Barn Dinner Show

Although it didn't last that long, I spent four delightful summers at the Bit-O-Wyo Ranch which was just a few miles from Curt Gowdy State Park. Dennis Coelho, Perry Jones, and I joined Dennis Steele and his family as they fed and entertained people from all over the world at the Horse Barn Dinner Show.

After a steak dinner with beans, baked potatoes, corn on the cob, and the rest of the fixings, we put on an hour-and-a-half family show, full of great music and hilarious comedy that included some audience participation. Many people who had been to other country dinner shows said that ours was by far the best. Dennis Steele was a real professional entertainer and Molly kept everyone in line. I would have liked to continue but 2012 would be my last summer. We moved to Arizona full-time later that year.

Bit-O-Wyo Horse Barn Dinner Show

Arizona

In 1994, Joanne and I bought a second home in an active adult community called PebbleCreek in Goodyear, Arizona. I had just sold the dealership a year earlier and Joanne had retired from teaching. We were looking for someplace to spend the winter months away from the wind and snow. I discovered PebbleCreek during a golf outing at the Wigwam Resort in February 1993. Even though the development was just getting off the ground, I could see the potential and knew of Ed Robson's successes in his other communities.

Joanne and I took a trip to Arizona during spring break of 1994 and purchased a lot. It was at the end of the Eagles Nest driving range and the patio faced the 10th fairway. We stood on that lot when there was nothing on that street and just a few houses a block away on hole number one.

Everyone who purchased a lot was given the option to delay building for up to one year. We settled on an Augusta model. We returned in January and went through the design process of choosing colors, cabinets, and other options. The house was finished, and we moved in July 1995. We were one of the first 200 homes built in PebbleCreek.

I played golf while Joanne tended to her flowers. Our two daughters, Susie and Cindy, and their families would come for a visit, usually during spring break or Thanksgiving. We would drive back to Cheyenne for Christmas and return in January. We remained snowbirds, traveling back and forth for eighteen years until we decided to go down to one home. In 2012 we sold our Cheyenne home and moved to Arizona full-time.

There weren't any music opportunities in PebbleCreek during those first few years, so I traveled all over the valley searching out the few festivals, jam sessions, and open mics that were available. Then when the community started to grow, a few clubs started to form.

My first involvement was with the PebbleCreek Singers. That's where I met Bruce Birnel, who a few years later would form the PebbleCreek Musicians. I joined Bruce for the first Burst Of Music concert, featuring the PebbleCreek Big Band, and would go on to perform with the Big Band for the next twelve years. I also became the treasurer of the Musicians Club.

Many talented people from all over the country started to move into PebbleCreek. Several had theater backgrounds and put on shows in the Eagles Nest Ballroom. They formed a new club called ShowTime. I played guitar for two of those first shows directed by my next-door neighbor, Vivian Ellison, and later performed in several ShowTime productions.

During the planning of the new Tuscany clubhouse, Ed Robson was going to include a small 50-seat auditorium that would be used as a lecture hall. Miriam Sweeney and Judy Alanzo met with Ed and convinced him to build the larger 330-seat performing arts theater. Thank goodness they did. PebbleCreek is one of the very few adult communities that has anything like the Renaissance Theater that we enjoy today. Between the Big Band, PebbleCreek Singers, and several ShowTime shows, I have spent many hours in that beautiful theater.

Later, I joined a folk group called The Desert Rovers. We performed for several years at local nursing homes, private home parties, and other outside events. We also organized an annual Folk Festival. The final group consisted of Dave Silverstein on banjo, Holly Carrier on guitar, Mike Caswell on mandolin, and me on guitar.

Desert Rovers: Dave Silverstein, Holly Carrier, Mike Caswell, Carl Halladay

Community Activities

Cheyenne Jaycees

Upon returning home and joining my father at the dealership, I started getting involved in civic activities. I joined and began attending meetings with the Cheyenne Junior Chamber of Commerce. The Jaycees, as they were called, were young and full of 'piss and vinegar'. Membership was between the ages of 21 and 35. They were just starting out in their jobs, careers, and marriages and were ready to make their mark on the world.

This was a very active time for the Jaycees. They were one of the largest clubs in Cheyenne and carried out several internal and external projects each year. Meetings were held in the basement of the Frontier Hotel. Shortly after I joined, they had a membership drive that brought the club to over 120 active members. I had only been a member for about two years when I was elected to serve on the board of directors.

It was at this time that the City of Cheyenne was making plans on how they were going to celebrate Cheyenne's Centennial year, 1867-1967. The Jaycees wanted to be part of this celebration. A former Jaycee president, Myron "Hoot" Wester, and a non-Jaycee, Gordon Wilson, came up with the idea that Cheyenne was born as an "end-of-track" town during the building of the transcontinental railroad and that the Jaycees could re-create a wild and woolly old west tent town as their contribution to the Centennial celebration. After several months and quite a bit of discussion, the Hell On Wheels project was adopted.

They got permission from the City of Cheyenne to put this tent town in Holliday Park. It consisted of ten tents that would be leased out to local merchants and the Jaycees coordinated daily shows and activities which included running a large beer tent called the Red Dog Saloon. It became one of the major tourist attractions of the summer. Hell On Wheels moved to other locations and continued for a few more years but finally ended when the Jaycees just ran out of gas.

One of my father's hobbies was photography, both stills and movies. He had just purchased a Kodak sound movie projector. You sent your developed 8mm film to Kodak and they installed a magnetic strip upon which you could record sound in sync with the movie. That process sounds ancient now but was state-of-the-art back in 1967. I took 20 rolls of 8mm film during the construction and operation of Hell On Wheels. After it was over, I recorded some audio from the Jaycees who had worked on the project, and I produced a twenty-two-minute documentary film. For many years following, I presented a program to clubs and organizations using the sound projector. I just recently had the film digitized and posted it on the Facebook page "You Know You're from Cheyenne if You Remember…" I donated the original film and sound projector to the State of Wyoming Archives.

The Jaycees kick you out when you reach 36 years old. Originally intended to be a young man's organization, they now accept women. After leaving, most of my fellow Jaycees joined the Cheyenne Kiwanis Club which had become one of the largest and most active Kiwanis clubs in the nation. I joined Rotary.

Cheyenne Civic Center

The City of Cheyenne broke ground on a new performing arts center in December 1977 and the premier opening of the new Cheyenne Civic Center took place on April 26, 1981. Many residents had been involved in the planning and promotion of this fine arts theater for Cheyenne. Mayor Don Erickson established the Gold Star Advisory Board. The 28 volunteer members handled a variety of duties from publicity and promotion to fund-raising and ticket sales. I chaired the business partnership sub-committee for several years and then became President of the Board in 1989.

Many celebrities have performed at our Cheyenne Civic Center over the years, but the highlight of my time on the board was when Joanne and I were asked to chauffeur Tony Bennett from the theater to Little America after his performance in 1991. Even though it was a short trip, we were able to visit with him one-on-one. He talked about his daughter Johanna and his current art projects. He even complained about the bumpy ride he had on the small commuter flight from Denver. If you are from Cheyenne, you've probably experienced that ride!

Sadly, Tony Bennett passed away at his home in New York City, on July 21, 2023, after being diagnosed with Alzheimer's disease. He was 96 years old.

Joanne and Carl Jr. with Tony Bennett

Equality State Bank

In 1977 my good friend Bill Bagley approached me about becoming involved in a new project that he and some of his friends were considering. A group of attorneys and businessmen had banded together and applied for a state charter to open a new independent bank in Cheyenne. Even though it sounded interesting, the timing couldn't have been worse. We were in the final stages of completing construction and about ready to move into our brand-new dealership building on Westland Road. So, I declined.

Five years later I was again invited to serve on the board of directors of Equality State Bank and I accepted. I was elected and served on the board from 1982 until it was sold to First Interstate Bank in 2000.

Mike Coughlin, President of the bank, and I became very good friends during my time on the board. We were part of a regular golf foursome that played at least once a week, mostly at the Cheyenne Country Club. We also occasionally traveled to play at several different courses in northern Colorado.

As a result of being on the board of directors of Equality State Bank, I had the opportunity to travel to golf outings in Arizona. Bankers Bank of the West, a correspondent bank for independent community banks, had many customers in Colorado, Wyoming, and Nebraska. Roger Reiling, their president, was an avid golfer and sponsored an annual golf outing for his clients at the Wigwam Golf Resort in Litchfield Park, Arizona. Mike and I and a few other directors attended several of these events. It was during our outing in 1993 that I discovered PebbleCreek. As I mentioned earlier, Joanne and I purchased a lot, built a home, and moved in July 1995.

After the bank was sold, Mike and Margo Coughlin purchased a lot and built a home in PebbleCreek and moved in, in 2001. They still have their home in Cheyenne but spend the winters here in Goodyear, Arizona.

Avis Rent-A-Car

RENT-A-CAR OPERATIONS are either run through corporate locations or as an independent franchised business. The licensees furnished their own fleet of cars. Operating one of these franchises had some definite advantages for an automobile dealer. They helped in obtaining additional car allotments, created a good stream of late model used cars, and helped to provide transportation if your car was in the shop.

For many years, the rental car businesses in Cheyenne were handled by three new car dealers. My father signed an Avis Rent-A-Car licensee agreement on May 1, 1968, and established an office in the Cheyenne Air Terminal.

Bill Dinneen, the Lincoln-Mercury dealer, had been the Hertz Rent-A-Car licensee for several years before our arrival. A few years later, Bill Tyrrell, the Chevrolet dealer, opened a Budget Rent-A-Car office at the airport.

Being number 2, we had to try harder. "We Try Harder" was one of the most successful advertising campaigns in history and is still remembered today. We had a heck of a time trying to keep enough of the free giveaway "We Try Harder" buttons available for customers.

Cassius Crow, who had recently retired from the Air Force, was our first Avis manager. He had one other counterperson to help but one or the other was always on call to meet late-arriving aircraft. I even spent a few days at the counter.

We were there for 25 years. It was a separate department of Halladay Motors and when I sold the business to Tim Joannides, he sold it back to Avis. Since then, it has been run as a corporate satellite location attached to Avis Rent-A-Car in Denver.

Fly Cheyenne

When the Airline Deregulation Act was passed in 1978, it ended price controls on airline tickets and mandatory routes that had previously been dictated by the Civil Aeronautics Board. This was devastating for many Wyoming communities. Some even lost their air service.

Cheyenne's air service weathered many years of steady decline until several concerned citizens banded together and formed Fly Cheyenne. As a result of being a rental car agent at the airport for several years and working closely with the airport manager, Jerry Olson, I was asked to serve on the board. Later I was elected to be chairman.

Through several avenues, print, radio, brochures, personal appearances, and even a billboard, we were able to get the word out about the value and convenience of using our air service. The 1991 figures marked a dramatic turnaround. The 28% increase in passenger boardings over the previous year was a far cry from the bleak trend of only a few years prior.

Deregulation did bring some benefits. For a short time, the competition between the two airlines servicing Cheyenne, United Express and Continental Express, resulted in 8 daily flights to and from Cheyenne with round-trip add-on rates as low as $20. Today we realize that those numbers could not be sustainable in the long run. Only 100 miles from Denver, Cheyenne's commercial air service has always been a difficult market to stabilize and probably always will be.

Fly Cheyenne Billboard

Oldsmobile

1944-2004

April 24, 2004, was a very sad day in automotive history. It was on that day that the last Oldsmobile rolled off the Lansing, Michigan assembly line.

Olds Motor Works was founded by Ransom E. Olds in 1897. In 1901, the company produced 425 cars making it the first high-volume gasoline-powered automobile manufacturer. During the years 1901 to 1904, the Curved Dash Oldsmobile was the first mass-produced car, made from the first assembly line, an invention that is often miscredited to Henry Ford and the Ford Motor Company. General Motors purchased the company in 1908.

Oldsmobile introduced the first fully automatic Hydramatic transmission in 1940 and the Rocket V8 engine in 1949. Over the years, they gave us iconic cars like the 88, 98, and front-wheel-drive Toronado. The Olds Cutlass became the best-selling car in the US in 1976 and continued into the 1980s.

Many factors led to the demise of the Oldsmobile line of automobiles. Rumors had circulated since the late 1980s that GM was considering discontinuing some of its product lines. Several models were built on the same chassis and produced on the same assembly line with only slight differences in the engines and designs. This was not "Your Father's Oldsmobile" and obviously, not your sons or daughters, either. The success of the Asian automobiles also added fuel to this fire especially when the Honda Accord and Toyota Camry evolved from compacts to mid-size models.

The official notice of the "phase out" of the Oldsmobile brand came on December 14, 2000. All the dealers and most of the buying public were devastated by this news. The last brand shelved by GM was the LaSalle, Cadillac's companion line, which expired in 1940. Our dealership survived the loss of Oldsmobile and it eventually worked out for the better, but it took several more years.

Oldsmobile's 100-Year Celebration

Oldsmobile was the first American car company to celebrate 100 years. The Centennial Celebration was held on August 20-23, 1997, in Lansing, Michigan. I attended that celebration.

It was a spectacular event with over 2,500 Oldsmobiles represented. Cross-country caravans sponsored by classic car clubs from around the United States and Canada arrived in Lansing to kick off the activities. On August 21st (actual birthday) a unique display of one vehicle for each production year was set up around the state Capitol. The remaining 2,400 Oldsmobiles were assembled by decade and displayed throughout the city in parks and large parking lots. I visited the R. E. Olds Transportation Museum and went on a General Motors Assembly Plant tour.

On the last day, we viewed a parade down Michigan Avenue to the State Capitol that included up to three Oldsmobiles for each production year. Also featured in the parade were over 70 Curved Dash Oldsmobiles, the company's iconic vehicle produced from 1901 to 1907.

In the evening, I attended the Oldsmobile Grand Finale at the Oldsmobile Main Stage featuring Randy Travis, Tammy Wynette, and fireworks. It was a great three days.

Olds 4-4-2

We have had many great memories and events over our sixty-year history as Cheyenne's Oldsmobile dealer, far too many to mention here but I would like to highlight a special Oldsmobile product and a special time that most of us old-timers will remember: The Oldsmobile 4-4-2.

The early 1960s became an era of muscle cars. Production of these cars was initiated by the increasing popularity of drag racing. Oldsmobile introduced the 4-4-2 in 1965 in response to their sister division Pontiac, which brought out the GTO a year earlier.

Mike Reid had developed a love of drag racing in high school and was currently one of the top salesmen on the Halladay Motors sales force. We had issued him a 4-4-2 as a demonstrator and sponsored his racing. Every weekend during the summer he would attend a race and return Monday morning with a trophy. Those trophies lined our showroom window for several years.

A paragraph from the summer of 1969 issue of our in-house newsletter the "Halladay Rocket Round-up", sums up Mike's accomplishments.

"At the present time, Reid holds the class record for F-stock in every drag strip in the Rocky Mountain area. He also holds the record for miles per hour in the E-classification for Division Five in the National Hot Rod Association. This division covers a seven-state area.

The class record that Reid holds was won in 1967 with an Olds 4-4-2 and still stands."

Tim Joannides recently added a 1970 4-4-2 W30 convertible to his classic car collection.

Bob Westbrook

I would like to spend a few minutes on a truly remarkable man. Bob Westbrook was a hot rodder and a good friend of mine. I met Bob when he first moved to Cheyenne in 1996. His reputation as one of the best luthiers (string instrument builder and repairman) in the Rocky Mountain area had preceded him. I introduced him to several of my friends in both the hot rod and music communities. Those first days I helped him become familiar with the city. He made his living repairing guitars, but his heart was in hot rodding.

He grew up in San Diego, California where, at an early age, got interested in building fast roadsters. He would race at all the lake meets and eventually, in 1965, won first place in his class D modified 1927 Ford roadster at the Bonneville Salt Flats. Bob was working for Don Vesco Motorcycles in 1970 as his crew chief when Vesco set a world speed record at 251.66 miles per hour driving his twin-engine streamliner "Big Red", becoming the first person to ride a motorcycle faster than 250 mph.

After moving to Cheyenne, Bob single-handedly built a 1927 Model T roadster pickup from the ground up, all while confined to a wheelchair. He started by modifying a 1929 Chevy frame, dropped in a brand new 385 Chevy racing engine, and finished up by building his unique hand controls. He even devised a sling on the end of an ATV wench with remote control, to lift him back into his wheelchair after working on the ground. Bob did ninety percent of the roadster by himself leaving only the painting and upholstering to other experts. On August 20, 2010, thirteen years after he started the project, he drove his dream car for the first time.

From an early age, he had suffered from a rare form of muscular dystrophy which he later learned was Charcot-Marie-Tooth disease. I would stop by a couple of times a week to take photos and keep tabs on his progress on the Roadster.

Everyone who ever knew Bob Westbrook was inspired by his dedication and ability to overcome obstacles. He didn't let his handicap get in the way. Bob passed away in October 2012.

Bob Westbrook and Roadster

Cadillac

1945-Present

My father had been in business for less than a year when he obtained the Cadillac franchise. In the summer of 1945, he was still operating out of the filling station on North Central Ave.

Because Cadillac wanted representation in towns too small to support a stand-alone dealer, they dueled up with other GM car divisions, and most often that was Oldsmobile. Some smaller towns represented all GM divisions under one roof. As a result, Cadillac established independent dealers as distributors. Our distributor was Rickenbaugh Cadillac in Denver. All cars were delivered by rail to the distributor where they would do the final service and allocate them to their dealers. There were few auto transports at that time, so most of the dealers would send salesmen to drive them back home from Denver. Cadillac distributors didn't last that long. By the early 1950s, all automobiles were being delivered to their door by auto transport.

*Carl Sr greeting automotive dignitaries at the Grand
Opening of our new dealership facilities, 408 E.
Lincolnway. My father shaking hands with Charlie
Guempelein, Oldsmobile Zone Manager with
Ralph Rickenbaugh (2nd from right) looking on.*

The Cadillac Eldorado Brougham

August 21, 1957, we delivered one of the most expensive cars sold
in Cheyenne. Alex Jensen had been a very good customer for
many years, buying a new Cadillac every year or two. That year
he made a special order request, and we sold him a brand-new
Cadillac Eldorado Brougham with a retail price of $13,074. In
2024 dollars that would be $141,767. It was one of only 400 built
that year. The car was $3,000 more than its closest US competitor
and was even more expensive at the time than a Rolls Royce.

The brushed stainless steel roof set the car apart. It had
unique center-opening doors that would lock when the car

was put in gear. Many other features that we consider standard today were cutting-edge then. They were all standard on the Eldorado Brougham. Air conditioning, 6-way memory power driver's seat, automatic headlight dimmer, automatic door locks, and a signal-seeking transistor radio with power antenna just to mention a few. The Eldorado Brougham was the world's first production car to have air suspension for a smoother ride and superior handling.

Luxury items included Mouton fur carpeting throughout. The glove compartment contained a fold-out shelf with a mirror, a matched set of magnetized silver tumblers, a cigarette case, a tissue dispenser, a lady's compact, and a unique lipstick and Arpege cologne in a special atomizer.

This was one of Harley Earl's (GM's design wizard) final creations before his retirement in 1958. Also, Fred Arnold, whom my father refers to in his time at the GM Proving Ground, was in charge of the engineering. It was designed to prove that Cadillac was indeed the luxury "Standard of the World," and we were fortunate to be able to sell one.

*Carl Sr delivering the 1957 Cadillac Eldorado
Brougham to Alex Jensen with John Lueras
and Bill Anderson looking on*

Tim Joannides located a 1957 Cadillac Eldorado Brougham that had been stored in a warehouse for 35 years. Al Benson drove to Denver from his home in Montrose, Colorado to inspect the car and reported to Tim, who was in Tucson, AZ at the time, that everything checked out. Tim then added this unique Cadillac to his classic car collection.

GMC Truck

1950-Present

We became a GMC Truck dealer in 1950. Back then the pickup truck was primarily a utility vehicle for farming, ranching, and the construction trades. Ford and Chevrolet led the truck field but this acquisition rounded out our line of vehicles so we could provide any type of transportation for our customers.

Today a pickup truck can be as luxurious as the highest-end automobile. This wasn't always the case but back in 1955, General Motors tried when they introduced their Chevrolet Cameo and GMC Town and Country Suburban. These models paved the way for today's Silverado and Sierra.

The Chevrolet Cameo was the first pickup truck with smooth rear fenders. They were only built for three years between 1955 and 1957. GMC Truck followed and came out with its version called the Town and Country Suburban. It was only in production for one year, 1956.

Even though this was an experiment it inspired other car-like features on pickup trucks, like the 1957 Ford Ranchero and then Chevy's own El Camino in 1959. Then by 1960, Dodge, Ford, and International had joined General Motors in making smooth-sided pickup trucks.

To my knowledge, we never sold a 1956 GMC Town and Country Suburban at the dealership; however, Tim Joannides located a fully restored one that he purchased and displayed for several years at the dealership. He sold the GMC and recently purchased a 1957 Chevrolet Cameo pickup.

Motor Homes

In 1972 we became a Sportscoach Motorhome dealer. Sportscoach was a class A motorhome with some distinctive features such as the aerodynamic pointed front end that set it apart from its competition. We introduced it as the "Cadillac of Motor Homes" with all the upgraded features as standard equipment on all models.

In the summer of 1973, my family planned a vacation to attend my wife's sister's wedding in Anaheim, California. We decided to fly out and then I would pick up a new Sportscoach at the factory in Chatsworth, California, and drive it back to Cheyenne.

Early one morning, my nephew drove me to Chatsworth, and I spent the rest of the day touring the factory. All went well until I left driving this huge motor home and hit the L.A. freeway (8 lanes) at rush hour. Not having a lot of experience driving motor homes, I held my breath for 2 and 1/2 hours till I reached my sister-in-law's home in Anaheim 58 miles away. I took the wrong exit which added 15 minutes to my trip. An experience I'll never forget.

The first few years it was received quite well, and we sold several units. Then in the late 70s, fuel shortages led to high gasoline prices, making such heavy gas users as RVs less attractive to the buying public. Moreover, high financing rates further dampened consumers' interest. We had sold our last Sportscoach before we moved to our new dealership on Westland Road.

Sportscoach

We never did get a franchise for the GMC Motor Home even though we tried. They were looking for someone who would commit to a full-blown RV dealership with sales and service facilities for several different brands including the GMC Motor Home.

Van Conversions

In the early 1980s cargo vans were converted into deluxe vehicles by independent companies. They were adding Captain's chairs, carpeting, interior lighting, and many more luxurious items. These van conversions were replacing the station wagon and rapidly becoming a family vehicle. They were a definite improvement over the "Hippie Vans" that preceded them.

Our first van conversions came from the Explorer Van Co of Warsaw, Indiana. With a crowded field at the time, they rose to the top by emphasizing quality and customer satisfaction. Originally, we had to order the van chassis, have it shipped to their factory, and then wait for it to be built. Later they were awarded a "bailment pool agent" by GMC, Chevrolet, and Ford. We could then order them directly from their finished stock. Explorer Vans were considered the 'Cadillac' of van conversions, and we were recognized as one of the top Explorer Van dealers in the US.

A few years later, we took on a less expensive van conversion line from Vanworks of Fort Collins, Colorado. We sold a lot of van conversions during this period and although they weren't motor homes, they helped fill that void. We also represented the Sherrod and Mark III conversion companies.

Medium Duty Trucks

Almost every GMC Truck dealer in the country was a Light Duty truck (standard line) franchised dealer. If they happened to have a customer who wanted to buy a Medium Duty truck, they could purchase it from a Medium Duty dealer. A few dealers elected to apply to General Motors for a Medium Duty Truck Franchise.

In our state, most of the business was gained through a bidding process with the respective government agencies, for example, heavy-duty dump trucks for snow removal and other construction projects for the Wyoming Highway Department or School Bus chassis for various school districts. These orders would come in as few as one or two or up to forty or fifty at a time. We ordered the chassis from GMC and specialized body companies would complete the orders.

Before Tim Joannides joined Halladay Motors, we had elected to stay out of this market. When Tim arrived, he immediately started to bid on these vehicles and obtained them through other franchised Medium Duty dealers. Within a short time, we were outselling our competition. It was then, in 1995, that we applied for and received a GMC Truck Medium Duty franchise.

We established a separate fleet and commercial truck sales office with the management and staffing of knowledgeable employees such as Bill Strickland and Ted Henry. We started to gain major inroads in the Cheyenne and regional medium-duty truck market in both retail and commercial.

We did very well in this market until General Motors reorganized its product lines and discontinued its medium-duty truck division due to the Chapter 11 bankruptcy in 2009.

The Datsun/Nissan Story

1964 - Present

My parents took a vacation trip to Hawaii after the N.A.D.A. convention in January of 1963. My father just happened to notice that all the taxis on Oahu were Japanese cars. Half were Toyotas and the other half had the nameplate "Bluebird", which he later discovered was a Datsun model. After returning home and trying to settle on a reliable entry-level car he immediately started to research the Datsun automobile.

In 1964 we became the second Datsun dealer in the Rocky Mountain area. Swede Ehrlich in Greeley, Colorado had preceded us by a few months. We sold seven cars in our first year but that was just the beginning. As it turned out, Datsun was a perfect fit for us. They were rapidly adding to their dealer base and establishing a strong foothold in the US for their share of the growing import market. For the next several decades our sales continued to improve, and we went head-to-head with other import dealers in our market area.

At the end of 1981, all Datsun dealers were informed that the company was changing the name of all its vehicles to Nissan. The rationale was that the name change would help the pursuit of a global strategy and identify more with the parent company. Other countries had been selling their cars under the Nissan badge for many years. The re-branding turned out to be very expensive. Changing the signs on 1100 dealerships, along with an extensive advertising campaign over the next four years, cost Nissan an estimated 500 million dollars.

MR. "K"

Yutaka Katayama, or Mr. K as he was fondly referred to by his employees and dealers alike, became a legend in the automobile industry. As a young rebel within the Nissan Corporation, he was banished to the United States, then a faraway outpost for the auto-maker. The year was 1960. But instead of being forgotten, the man turned the company into a global player. He traveled all over the country signing up dealers. As president of Nissan Motor Corp. U.S.A., he built his dealership network and then fought hard with Japan to supply them with cars suited for the US market. In the late 1960's he balked at the plan to market the new sports car in the US under the Japanese name "Fairlady." Thank goodness he did. The 240Z would become one of the most popular and affordable sports cars of the era.

My parents became good friends with Mr. K even though they only met one or two times a year at conventions or announcement meetings. For several years my mother and Mr. K exchanged small gifts (a Japanese tradition) at the annual N.A.D.A. conventions.

My parents also extended him an invitation to come to our Cheyenne Frontier Days celebration. He accepted, not once but twice. The first time was in 1972 and he had so much fun that he brought his wife with him on the second trip in 1976. The Nissan party consisted of Mr. Katayama, Chairman of the Board Nissan Motor Corp. U.S.A., and his wife Masako; Mr. S. Kosaka, Assistant to V.P. Sales; Bob Bower, Denver Zone Manager; and Lee Jousma, District Sales Manager.

They spent three days taking in the sights and sounds of "The Daddy Of Em All." During their visit to the rodeo, the announcer re-named one of the bulls Mr. Katayama, as was customary to recognize dignitaries in the audience.

Mr. K remarked in his thank you letter, *"I received a real surprise by seeing a bull by the name of Mr. Katayama. Surprisingly, I was so strong that I even threw off the professional cowboy."*

Another highlight of their trip was a reception the night of their arrival at my parent's home on 8th Avenue. Mr. Kosaka wrote after returning home,

"This was my first time to have seen the real "Westerners and Cowboys." It was a real excitement to see the chuck wagon race, the parade, and the rodeo at the heart of the Wild West. However, more excitement was that I would meet you and your family and could have such a nice time at your beautiful house. I will never forget that night as one of the most joyful times in my life."

Gordon Whitby, Western Sales Director for Nissan, wrote in his memoirs "Earning The American Dream"

"Though I worked for Nissan for seventeen years, the one period I am especially proud of is the years 1969 through 1976 working with Mr. Katayama. Mr. K took great pride in what we had accomplished in the West. He often made it a point to travel with me, as he thoroughly enjoyed meeting his Western dealers at their dealerships.

One such trip was when Mr. K was presented with a Stetson cowboy hat by our Cheyenne dealer Carl Halladay, who arranged for Mr. K to become a Cheyenne Deputy Sheriff with his own Sheriff's star. He was then escorted in a stagecoach around the Cheyenne Frontier Days stadium by real cowboys. He often told me that it was one of his most memorable trips."

In 1977, a year after his trip to Cheyenne, Mr. K was called back to Japan to finish out his career with Nissan. He passed away on February 19, 2015, at the age of 105.

Super Bowls

Nissan was a major NFL Super Bowl sponsor for many years. Each year they held a national sales contest and rewarded their best dealers with a trip to the Super Bowl. Every year we were consistently in the top ten percent of the dealers in our market area. I was very fortunate to win first place and attend three of the Nissan Super Bowl Spectacular contests, in 1985, 1987, and 1990.

The first one I attended, Super Bowl XIX, was played at the Stanford, California stadium. Nissan chartered a mid-sized cruise ship, docked in San Francisco which became our hotel room for the next 5 days. It was complete with on-ship and on-shore activities, culminating with the football game. Joanne was teaching during that first trip in 1985 and couldn't take the time off so I took our top salesman, Lee Tafoya.

Lee, being an avid golfer, suggested that we take our clubs. After we arrived aboard the ship, the cruise director made us a tee time at a local course so we could play a round instead of spending our free day shopping.

That day, Lee and I left the boat, hailed a cab, and true to form, Lee couldn't quite remember the name of the course or how to get there. The cab driver drove around for a while and then took us to where he thought we wanted to go. We ended up arriving at the private, exclusive, military-only golf club at The Presidio, in a cab! The greeter said we must be in the wrong place and tried to have us turn around, but Lee with his persuasive 'gift of gab' got us in. With a few extra dollars to the starter, we were paired up with a couple of retired colonels and had a great day. Oh yes, the 49ers beat the Dolphins 38-16.

Joanne and I attended the next two. 1987 Super Bowl XXI at the Rose Bowl in Pasadena, California (New York Giants 39, Denver Broncos 20). Then in 1990, we attended Super Bowl XXIV at the New Orleans Superdome. Talk about embarrassing, it was the biggest blowout in Super Bowl history. The San Francisco 49ers beat the Denver Broncos 55 to 10.

Upon leaving the New Orleans Superdome, after that devastating defeat, Joanne wanted to trade in her Denver Bronco T-Shirt for a Joe Montana one.

These were truly 'Spectacular' trips!

Other Imports

IN 1950, A GERMAN COMPANY began selling its iconic car in the United States. Much like the Beatles would soon lead the 'British Invasion', the Volkswagen Beetle began the 'Import Auto Invasion'. For the next several years the European automakers aggressively sought out established dealers to introduce their automobiles to the American buyer. The Japanese wouldn't enter the market for another ten years.

During this time, between 1957 and 1962, we became the dealer for several European cars and trucks. Among them were Renault (French), Hillman (British), Land Rover (British), Peugeot (French), Borgward (German), and Citroen (French). My records show that during these six years, we sold 132 imported vehicles. We only sold a few of each of these brands. Most of the European auto manufacturers had not established a sound foothold in the U.S. When something broke down it was weeks before the parts would arrive from overseas. The most popular of these imports were the Hillman Minx and the Land Rover (Jeep style).

Lee Tafoya is at the wheel of a new Hillman Roadster while Carl Sr. looks on.

Short-Lived Daewoo

Now fast forward to April 2000. We were one of the first dealers in the country to sign with Daewoo. The South Korean automaker was approaching bankruptcy due to labor and financial problems when General Motors stepped in and purchased half of its assets. With this optimism, the US dealer body grew to 525 franchises. It was thought that these cars could compete with Kia and Hyundai. GM, however, was on a different path and eventually stopped importing the vehicle. By 2002 they continued to produce entry-level automobiles but only for Asian markets.

New Car Announcement Day

A GREAT DEAL OF EXCITEMENT was generated throughout the automotive world each year with the fall introduction of the new models. After WWII and through the 1960s, every US manufacturer changed their body styles, added chrome, introduced different colors and trims, upgraded engines, and added new accessories almost every year. It was a period when you could actually tell the make and year of a car from a block away. Dealers would keep the new cars hidden in barns, garages, or other undisclosed locations until they went on display on that special ANNOUNCEMENT DAY!

We held a special invitation-only New Car Announcement Party for all our previous customers every year during the 1940s, '50s, and '60s. They were always very well attended and yes, sometimes we covered up the windows!

*Announcement Party introducing the
1966 Oldsmobile Toronado*

Shortly after Tim Joannides joined Halladay Motors, he organized annual preview parties at large hotel banquet rooms. They were initially held at the Hitching Post Inn and later at the Holiday Inn. We spent the entire day preparing and transporting over 30 vehicles to the venue. Previous customers, dignitaries, and the press all received special invitations to this lavish party. None of the other Cheyenne dealers were doing anything close, and it was the talk of the town for many weeks after.

This harkened back to the time when my father was in charge of putting on auto shows for GM, at the Waldorf Astoria and the Conrad Hilton. The more things change, the more they stay the same.

Advertising and Promotions

THE MOST IMPORTANT THING, in any retail business, is to keep your name and products in front of the public. The year after we arrived in Cheyenne, 1945, there were 18 new car dealers. My father needed to establish his business as fast as possible. Advertising accomplished that.

There were two newspapers in Cheyenne when we arrived. The Wyoming Eagle (morning edition) and the Wyoming State Tribune (evening edition). Even though it was more expensive, our ads always appeared in both papers. Some dealers elected to only advertise in the more widely read evening edition.

From the very beginning, my father incorporated the phrase "Today It's Halladay" in our logo and advertising. We've also capitalized on another well-known name and advertised "Doc

Halladay" (not Holliday). We have also used the phrase "Every Day's A Halladay." We've had a lot of fun with these over the years.

Notable Campaigns

Miss Wyoming Pageant... For several years during the 1960s, Oldsmobile sponsored the national Miss America Pageant. Oldsmobile made a fleet of cars available to the dealership in the town where the state pageant was held. Each contestant was issued a brand-new convertible to drive during the week-long event. The winner of the state pageant was issued a car to drive for the year of her reign.

*Carl Sr. sitting in a 1963 Oldsmobile Convertible
with the Miss Wyoming contestants*

Darth Vader... Children of all ages got a real treat in October 1982 when they got to see up close, the real Darth Vader, or at least the stunt man that portrayed him in a few scenes in the Star Wars movies. Terry Kelly had performed some sword fighting (lightsaber) scenes in the first three movies and was on tour making personal appearances.

He appeared in the dealership showroom on October 4th and 5th for four shows each day. In addition to the shows, he and his sidekick Chris Clark, stunt man for Dukes of Hazzard, visited children at Stride Learning Center, Memorial Hospital, and Goins Elementary School. At each appearance, they were accompanied by two Jawas played by James Smith and Gary Keith, two kids from Cheyenne.

Over 1,000 Cheyenne children will never forget the time they met one of film history's most menacing villains.

Darth Vader

Don't You Buy No Ugly Truck… This campaign hit the newspaper and airways with a "Bang!" A little old lady in a sloppy dress and bonnet would holler the slogan "Don't You Buy No Ugly Truck" and encourage you to buy a GMC Truck from Halladay Motors. Needless to say, it got a lot of push-back from all of the English teachers.

Doc Halladay's Gang… This was another theme we used several times. The salesmen would all dress up in Western attire (outside of Frontier Days) and rope a good deal for the customer. The play on the name "Doc Halladay" (not Holliday) was remembered long after the promotion was over.

Larry Birleffi and the Renault

Anyone living in Wyoming from the late 1940s through the 1990s would recognize the name Larry Birleffi as the voice of the Wyoming Cowboys. He broadcasted all the University of Wyoming football and basketball games, both home and away, on KFBC radio. He also wrote a weekly sports column for the Wyoming Tribune Eagle.

One day he approached my father with the idea of starting an early morning talk show on KFBC radio. My dad thought it was a great idea and helped Larry launch his long-running program Cheyenne Today as its major sponsor.

Several years later, right after we had taken on the Renault franchise, Larry was looking for a second car. On one of his sales trips to the dealership, my dad told Larry that he would give him a good deal on a new Renault and sponsor his program if he would periodically give live reports on the air about what he thought of the car.

Fred McCabe was the General Manager of the newspaper. He had a great sense of humor and was a real jokester. Larry would stop by the newspaper to write his sports column and park his car a half block away in a parking lot at 17th and Warren.

Well, Fred hired this kid, gave him a 5-gallon can of gas, and told him, "Whenever you see that Renault parked there you fill it up to the top."

In my recorded interview with Larry, he said,

"I couldn't figure out why the gas gauge wouldn't move. I even pounded on the dash, but I couldn't get it to go down an inch. I even talked to my filling station people, and they said it was full. I was getting 40, 50, 60 miles to the gallon, maybe 100. I never needed any gas. I don't remember how long this went on, but it was way over a month. This also worked its way into my radio reporting, this marvelous French car that didn't use any gas. I had no idea what was happening. They had me hook, line, and sinker."

Fred then got the kid to start taking some gas out. This would have been quite a story if it had continued but Larry said that he caught the young man in the act. Then Fred and my father, who was a co-conspirator, fessed up and they all had a good laugh.

Larry had purchased almost all his cars from our dealership. Starting with an Oldsmobile 76. Then 88's, 98's, and his favorite the Toronado. He also owned one of Cadillac's entry-level luxury cars called the Cimarron.

Larry Birleffi passed away in 2008 at the age of 90. Even though he had spent his 50-year career speaking on radio and television, he always got the name of his Cadillac wrong. He would refer to it as his "Cinnamon."

Larry Birleffi interviewing Carl Sr. at a New Car Showing

Passing the Torch

IN THE SUMMER OF 1987, I was looking to hire a General Manager.
I had placed an ad in our national trade paper: Automotive News.
Tim Joannides called one day and after a brief conversation, we
agreed to meet. Tim was working as General Manager at Tyrrell
Chevrolet since moving to Cheyenne from Tucson, Arizona in
1983. I was aware of the great job he had done with Chevrolet
and after doing some research I was confident that he would be
a good fit for our dealership.

We knew that if anyone saw us together in Cheyenne the
rumors would start flying so we decided to meet for lunch in Fort
Collins. Tim shared his automotive and family history with me.
It became obvious that he could not reach his goal of becoming a
dealer if he remained at Tyrrell's and he was considering moving
away from Cheyenne to find an opportunity somewhere else.
We agreed to meet again in a couple of weeks. We also discussed
the possibility that after a few years, if we were both comfortable

with each other and his progress, he would have the opportunity to buy into the dealership.

I didn't have any family members who had ever shown an interest in the dealership. My two daughters were never involved, and my handicapped son was living in a group home in Sheridan, Wyoming. I probably would have sold the dealership at some later date, but this opportunity was available now. And it all worked out great.

Tim gave his notice to Tyrrell Chevrolet and came to work as General Manager of Halladay Motors on July 7, 1987. He hit the ground running!

In the next four and a half years, Tim proved that he was more than capable of running the dealership. He was well-received and respected by all the employees. He met and exceeded his goals in all phases of the operation. He was also one of the most organized people I have ever known. Long before "smart phones," Tim was never seen without his handwritten Day-Timer, reminding him what would happen today, tomorrow, next week, next month, and even next year, and he still uses it today!

Tim and I entered into a Buy-Sell Agreement on December 4, 1992. I had a ten-year employment agreement and retained ownership of the real estate. Eventually, Tim purchased the main location on Westland Road and then the old building (on the cover) at 500 East Lincolnway where he currently operates the Halladay Motors Collision Center.

When my employment agreement ended, in December 2002, I was no longer eligible to have a demonstrator and so for the first time in my life, I had to BUY a car. Not only one car but two. One for my wife. That always brings a chuckle from my friends who say, "Now you know what we go through!"

Tim and I at the closing with Tom Long, Mike McGee, and Peter Arnold looking on.

Tim Joannides

Tim was born in Rock Island, Illinois. His father, Louis had immigrated from the island of Cyprus in 1930 and married Jennie, a Greek American in 1938. His father was in the insurance business, but Tim was interested in automobiles. He worked for dealers in Illinois and Tucson, Arizona before accepting a position with Tyrrell Chevrolet in Cheyenne in 1983.

When Tim moved to Cheyenne, he immediately became involved in several community activities including the Saints Constantine and Helen Greek Orthodox Church. Shortly after arriving, he helped re-organize and manage the Greek Festival held every year and took it to a new level. He is a Past President of AHEPA Cowboy Chapter #211, a national Hellenic fraternal organization.

Fourteen years ago, he initiated an annual AHEPA fundraising golf tournament, and two years ago, started the Cars, Cigars, & Guitars Classic Car Show. Tim is very proud of his heritage as demonstrated by the GREEK lapel pin that he wears every day.

Tim and Kathy Swegle were married on June 6, 1985. Tim has three children from a previous marriage, Chris, Nick, and Angelia. He and Kathy had one son, Andrew.

Kathy Joannides passed away on May 13, 2023, after a four-year battle with ALS.

Chris Joannides joined his father at the dealership in 1989. He had previous automotive experience in Illinois and Colorado before coming to Cheyenne. He worked his way up from Used Car Manager to General Manager in 2001. Chris had completed the NADA Dealer Candidate Academy and was in line to take over the operation at some future date. This, however, didn't happen. Due to some medical issues, Chris resigned his position at Halladay Motors on October 5, 2006. He and his wife, Betsey, and three children, currently reside in Fort Smith, Arkansas, where he has settled in on a successful career as director of Hope Campus, a homeless shelter.

Tim's mother, Jennie Joannides moved to Cheyenne in 1996 to be closer to her family. Three years after they were married, she and her husband, Lieutenant Louis Joannides were living near Hickam Field in Oahu, Hawaii during the Pearl Harbor invasion.

After moving to Cheyenne, she gave speeches throughout the area about her experiences and what she saw during and after the attack. She was very independent and proud that she lived by herself and was driving into her mid-90s. She passed away at age 100.

Tim has way too many experiences, accolades, awards, and recognitions to mention them all here. Maybe we will get the whole picture and "the rest of the story" when he writes his own memoir.

The Amazing Suzuki Story

1992-2009

Before I begin, I want to give Tim Joannides 100% credit for the magnificent success of the Suzuki introduction to our market.

Late in 1991, Suzuki was looking to expand their dealer base and was interviewing several dealers in our market area. Tim approached me with the idea of taking on this line of entry-level cars and SUVs. His research revealed that one-third of the automobile registrations in Laramie County were compact or sub-compact vehicles. Twenty-seven years earlier we had taken on Datsun to fill this void but over time Datsun/Nissan cars had grown bigger and more expensive and didn't serve that purpose anymore. It wasn't that hard to sell me on the idea, so I gave him the green light and said he could run with it. And boy did he!

He put in our application, and we were chosen as the dealer to represent Suzuki for the state of Wyoming. Tim put in an initial order for 66 vehicles. He immediately began a media teaser campaign that Halladay Motors was coming out with brand-new front-wheel-drive, fuel-efficient cars for under six grand and brand-new four-wheel-drives for under seven grand, without mentioning the name of the product. The advertising blitz started on "Super Bowl Sunday" and continued to saturate Cheyenne and much of the rest of the state.

Tim started sending out press releases the week before the January 30th grand opening alerting the region's media that something new was coming and extending an invitation to a sneak preview party the day before the opening. Invitations were also sent to all managers of the local financial institutions including credit unions and banks. A few days later, a direct mailer went to 22,000 households in the Cheyenne area. This was accompanied by extensive large-format advertising in all the newspapers throughout the state, finally showing the vehicles with some extremely low, attractive introductory prices.

The VIP party for the press and dignitaries went fabulously, with some 120 people attending. Gifts were given to everyone as they entered, and the products were nicely displayed throughout the dealership and were attended by extensively trained sales personnel. Also in attendance were representatives of the American Suzuki Motor Corp. The event created an abundance of media coverage extending throughout the following weeks.

Tim and Carl, Jr. with the first
four transports of Suzukis.

In the first full month, February 1992, we delivered 58 Cars and trucks and became the No.1 Suzuki dealer in the United States.

We beat out the top dealer in the country, Miami, Florida by 6 units. We delivered more units in February than the next four dealers in the L.A. Region combined. We finished out the year in the top 10 of 330 dealers nationally. This was indeed the most successful product launched in Halladay Motors' history, all due to Tim Joannides' vision and hard work.

General Motors' "Musical Chairs"

GENERAL MOTORS, AND IN FACT, all automobile manufacturers, has a great deal of control as to whom it wants to have as its dealers. It's called the "Selling (franchise) Agreement." The manufacturer initially decides where they want to be located and requires the dealer to provide adequate facilities, working capital, and staffing to represent their product. This sounds reasonable but as demographics and markets change over time, the manufacturer may insist that the dealer make changes that he can't or won't do.

One good example is when we initially took on Datsun/Nissan in 1964 we sold a total of 7 cars that first year. By the time we moved to Westland Road in 1979, we were selling over 30 a month. More than enough to justify and support a stand-alone building but we were still selling them from the GM store. We would eventually need an exclusive dealership facility to sell Nissan.

Back in 1996, General Motors announced that they intended to reduce their dealership roster from 9,000 to 7,000 and consolidate several product lines under a program called Project 2000. Dealers were up in arms and didn't want to be forced to sell their dealership, especially to a competitor. A town the size of Cheyenne was slated to have two GM dealers, but the problem, at that time, was that there were three willing buyers but no willing sellers.

General Motors has had its ups and downs over its 114-year history. It made it through the Great Depression and rose to become the model of an American corporation. At one point in the 1950s, one of every two cars sold in the United States carried a GM brand name. However, it got too big and didn't keep pace with changing markets, and in 2009 it had to file for Chapter 11 bankruptcy.

They used the trip into bankruptcy court to shed plants, dealerships, debt, and other liabilities they could no longer afford. The much smaller "New GM." ended up with four car brands for sale in the US, Chevrolet, Cadillac, GMC Truck, and Buick.

Buick — Pontiac

In August of 2003, Tim Joannides, General Motors, and John Dinneen, finally came to an agreement for Tim to purchase the Buick and Pontiac franchises with the possibility of obtaining Subaru at a later date. Along with this agreement came the requirement that we would only sell General Motors cars and trucks from our 2100 Westland Road location.

The blueprint of what GM envisioned for Cheyenne dealers in the 1990s finally came to pass. Buick and Pontiac filled the void left by the loss of Oldsmobile. Little did we know at that time that in six short years, Pontiac and GMC Truck Medium Duty franchises would be another casualty of General Motors' reorganization.

Expansion

TIM JOANNIDES HAD AGREED that our 2100 Westland Road dealership facility would only sell GM products and the next few years would bring a flurry of building and reorganization for Halladay Motors. He immediately went on a search to find locations for Nissan and Suzuki.

During this same period, 2005, Tim spent a lot of time and money remodeling the old dealership building at 510 E. Lincolnway into a state-of-the-art collision and paint center. We were running out of room on Westland Road and the move downtown tripled the size of our body shop. Our vacated body shop space was converted into a used car detail area and additional stalls to service medium-duty trucks.

The New Nissan Building,
1880 Westland Road, 2005–Present

There wasn't much land left on Westland Road, but we got lucky. The Rocky Mountain Health Club was about a block away and had been closed for over a year. Tim was able to purchase that property and after the building was razed, he built the new Nissan dealership. Pappas and Pappas were the architects and Edwards Construction was the general contractor. This corporate-identified Nissan building was long overdue. Two of the other major import cars, Honda, and Toyota, owned by the Chevrolet and Ford dealers, were already operating from their own stand-alone facilities on Westland Road.

We opened in October 2005 and our sales immediately increased.

2006-2023 Suzuki / Subaru

In 1997, Tim Joannides purchased the property at the northeast corner of Lincolnway and Westland Road. The previous owner had been operating a used car lot there, and we established our Bargain Corner and opened a Buy Here – Pay Here lot for our budget-priced used cars.

Within two years of obtaining Buick and Pontiac, Tim purchased the Subaru franchise from Dinneen. A new building was built at 1615 Westland Road to accommodate both Suzuki and Subaru. The dual-built concept included separate show-rooms for each vehicle with common parts and service area in the middle. The lot was quite small and created some problems in limiting the number of vehicles we could display for both products.

In September 2009, the Halladay Motors management team decided to terminate its Suzuki franchise, due to declining sales and service revenues of the brand. The facility then became an exclusive Subaru dealership.

After Jim Casey took the reins of the Halladay Auto Group, he immediately started researching the possibilities of building a new home for our rapidly growing Subaru line of cars. The ideal location, as it turned out, was right next door to the GM dealer-ship. Many years earlier, we had purchased the adjacent vacant land with just this thought in mind.

In March of 2022, plans were being drawn up to build a new dealership facility. Between architects, builders, and Subaru, the state-of-the-art Halladay Subaru dealership building took shape at 2030 Westland Road and was completed in October 2023.

The previous Suzuki/Subaru building at 1615 Westland Road has been converted into a Mobil-1 Care Center and a retail auto-mobile reconditioning service center.

Suzuki – Subaru Building, 1615 Westland Road

Awards and Recognitions

Time Magazine Quality Dealer Award

Each year, Time Magazine, along with the National Automobile Dealers Assn. (NADA) recognizes a select few new car franchised dealers to receive its prestigious Quality Dealer award. Dealers are selected after submitting a comprehensive 20-page entry form outlining exceptional dealership performance along with distinguished community service. A panel from the University Of Michigan Graduate School Of Business Administration reviews each entry and approves each dealer. Recipients from Wyoming have always been nominated by their fellow dealers and sponsored by our state association, Wyoming Automobile Dealers Assn., WADA.

Three of the four dealer principals of Halladay Motors have received the Time Magazine Quality Dealer Award. I was nominated by the Wyoming Automobile Dealers Association and received the award in 1992 at the NADA Convention in Dallas Texas. Twenty-one years earlier, my father, Carl Sr., received the award in 1971 which was presented to him at the San Francisco convention. Tim Joannides also received this award at the NADA convention in Orlando, Florida in 2000.

Carl Jr., Time Magazine Quality Dealer Award

Just before going to press, I was informed that Jim Casey had been selected to receive this award, now called 'Time Dealer of the Year'. He will be presented with the award at the NADA convention in New Orleans on January 25, 2025.

The Dewar Trophy

Cadillac set the world's standard for high quality in 1908 by earning the Dewar Trophy presented by England's Royal Automobile

Club. The automakers' actions in accomplishing this would seem trivial today but at the time they represented far-reaching advances in engineering, even encouraging the evolution of what became today's Society of Automotive Engineers (SAE) International.

Henry Leland, one of Cadillac's founders, encouraged standardization as a company priority. His background was in machine tools and firearms manufacture, where precision was paramount and interchangeable parts made their first appearance.

In 1908 three Cadillac Model K cars were shipped to England where they were completely disassembled, and all the parts were scrambled into a pile of 2163 pieces. They were reassembled and the three cars proceeded to complete a 500-mile road trip after which Cadillac was awarded the Dewar Trophy for this impressive display of parts interchangeability. The judges declared Cadillac "Standard of the World", a motto that still lives today.

Cadillac used a replica of this trophy to recognize a select few dealers for outstanding achievements in all dealership departments and for full certification in their Complete Customer Satisfaction System. Halladay Motors met all the rigorous requirements and was awarded the Trophy on March 30, 1994. That year only 160 of the 1,500 Cadillac dealers received the Dewar Trophy Award. It is still proudly displayed in our Cadillac showroom.

BBB Torch Award for Ethics

From the very beginning in 1944, Carl Halladay, Sr. developed a strong reputation for fair dealing and good customer service. That same reputation has carried on and strengthened through four owners and in 2019 Halladay Motors was awarded the Better Business Bureau Torch Award for Ethics. Jim Casey accepted the award from the BBB Foundation serving Northern Colorado and Wyoming.

Upon receiving the award Casey said, "It was very humbling to receive the award and it is an affirmation of our company's values. The cornerstone of our business is ethics and integrity." Casey said he believes integrity begins with how a business treats its employees, customers, and the community it serves.

We have received many awards including GMC Truck Leaders of Distinction, Oldsmobile Elite, Wyoming's first GM Certified Used Car Dealer, Suzuki Directors Club, and many more. Being a good automobile dealer always brings recognition from the manufacturer, but we don't do it for recognition. We do it because it's the right way to do business.

Industry & Dealer Relations

YEARS AGO, MY FATHER SAID, "The automobile dealer will be the last independent merchant on main street." That statement is becoming truer each year as 'big box' stores and conglomerates keep eating up the mom-and-pop businesses throughout the country.

The automobile dealer is unique in that he operates several businesses under one roof. New car sales, used car sales, service, parts, and sometimes a body shop. These not only require bricks and mortar facilities but hands-on management by an owner with a vested interest in its success. Over the years, many automobile manufacturers have tried to market their products and have failed every time. Private ownership, through the dealership franchise system, has survived for over 100 years and is still the best way to sell cars one at a time at retail.

That said, it is vital that the line of communication remains strong between the dealer and the manufacturer. It is in their best interest, as well as the dealers' because they are dependent on each other. That's where the Dealer Councils come in.

Dealer Councils

All automobile manufacturers have periodic meetings with dealer representatives, usually once a year to review future plans, discuss grievances, and generally try to improve on their mutual goals.

My father, myself, and Tim Joannides have served on many dealer councils. We were the voice representing our fellow dealers with the manufacturers of the many different automobiles that we handle.

The one my father was most proud of was when he was invited to serve on the General Motors Presidents Dealer Advisory Council. In 1958 and 1959, he was one of eighteen to represent over 16,000 dealers. While all other dealer council representatives are elected by their fellow dealers, participation in this council is a result of a personal invitation from the president of General Motors.

Dealer Associations

ALL BUSINESSES BENEFIT from getting together with others in their industry and the automobile business is no exception. Many things can be accomplished through local, state, and national associations.

Cheyenne Automobile Dealers

As I had mentioned earlier, when my father arrived in Cheyenne there were fourteen new car dealers. At that time the Cheyenne Automobile Dealers was a committee of the Cheyenne Chamber of Commerce but later it became its own association. The dealers would meet once a month, usually for lunch and to review any local issues that affected their business.

Putting on a joint auto show was one of the main activities of the association. Most of these shows were held indoors in the fall to introduce the new models. For a few years, we held outdoor shows in the spring. The parking lot at the Wyoming

Tribune-Eagle newspaper building was a very popular site, but we always took a chance on the weather.

As the dealer body dwindled, fewer and fewer meetings were held. Auto shows were becoming a thing of the past. Dealers were getting their information from other automotive sources eliminating the need to get together and as a result the Cheyenne Automobile Dealers Association officially disbanded on January 1, 2021.

1954 Cheyenne Automobile Dealers. Back row from left: Ike Spratt, Dodge – D.E. Taylor, Pontiac – Carl Halladay, Olds, Cadillac, GMC Truck – Jim Walton, Ford – Ace Tyrrell, Chevrolet – Bill Dinneen, DeSoto, Plymouth. Seated: Gus Fleischli, Studebaker – Keith Sutherland, Packard – George Cropper, Nash – Otis Melton, Buick – Temp Templin, Lincoln, Mercury – Not pictured Roy Manners, Chrysler, Plymouth

Wyoming Automobile Dealers Association

The Wyoming Automobile Dealer Association (WADA) has represented new car and truck franchised dealers throughout the state since 1935. They keep the members abreast of important issues including pending state and federal legislation, insurance programs, industry relations, and various programs of interest to the dealers.

Many things have changed in the 89 years since WADA was formed. The most obvious is the number of dealerships operating in Wyoming. There used to be a dealer representing almost every major brand of car in every town, but through attrition and consolidation, those numbers have been dramatically reduced. Small towns were hit the hardest when their sales volume couldn't justify keeping the doors open. There is no longer a new car dealer in Douglass, Buffalo, Sundance, Worland, and many other small Wyoming towns. Established dealers eventually bought out other dealers in their town and some even expanded into other communities.

Marsha Allen has been with WADA since 1989 and has been the Executive Director for the past sixteen years. She told me in a recent conversation that when she started there were over 120 dealers. Today there are 48 member dealerships in Wyoming controlled by 30 dealer principals.

Even though there are fewer individual dealers, the sales volume and products represented have increased. In 2020, Wyoming's new car dealers generated 1.6 billion dollars in sales, a 68 percent increase over the previous 10 years. Those sales created over 91 million dollars in state sales tax paid. 2,100 employees earned over 116 million dollars in wages which contributed an additional $23 million in state and federal income taxes paid. Our automobile dealers help to keep our state economy healthy and contribute to its success.

Officers and directors are elected each year at the annual convention. Since 2001 they now serve a two-year term. My father served as WADA President for the 1956 term. I was President in 1978 and Tim Joannides served when they changed to a two-year term. He was President 2007-2008. Jim Casey is currently the President of the Wyoming Automobile Dealers Association.

National Automobile Dealers Association

When someone mentions NADA the first thing that probably comes to mind for the average old-timer is the used-vehicle valuation guide. This little orange book has been around since 1933 and was compiled from thousands of used car sales by member dealers and other sources and published in different regions of the United States. In 2015, J.D. Power purchased NADA's Used Car Guide division. The printed consumer guide has been discontinued but used car values are still available on their website.

Our national association is so much more than that little orange book. NADA is the "Voice of the Dealer," and has represented their interest, the interests of their employees, and their customers for over 100 years. They represent more than 16,000 new-car dealers and advocate on their behalf before all branches of the federal government, manufacturers, the media, and the public.

Training and Education

 Successfully running an automobile dealership can be very complicated. It's like managing four or five separate businesses at the same time. Someone who has the means and desire to become a dealer principal most likely had most of his automotive experience in the sales department but doesn't have a clue about service or parts. This is where NADA comes in. They have been running a very successful Dealership Academy for many years. This is a very comprehensive program teaching all phases of an automobile dealership.

Both Chris Joannides and Jim Casey completed this program. It starts with a week of in-person school followed by a year of monthly in-dealership lessons and assignments. By the time you graduate, you have all the tools needed to be a successful dealer. It's all up to you.

NADA didn't have this program available in 1965 when I started. I did, however; attend a seven-week Dealership Management school at the General Motors Institute in Flint, Michigan. It covered the same information as the NADA program.

NADA 20 Groups

Even after you have had all the training and settled into running the day-to-day operation there are still some unanswered questions. How am I doing compared to other dealers? Where do I need to improve? It's hard to operate in a vacuum. NADA addresses these concerns with its 20 Groups.

NADA established several dealership analysis groups called 20 Groups. Each group consists of 20 dealers of similar size (sales volume), handling similar products (GM duels, etc.) in communities far enough apart that they were not in competition with each other. My first NADA 20 group was a Cadillac-Oldsmobile group.

Every month each dealer would submit their financial statement and within 10 days we would receive a comprehensive report listing how we stacked up against our fellow dealers on almost every financial statement line from every department. We could see how we were doing by comparison and take action if it needed correction.

An in-person meeting would be held two or three times a year to review these reports in depth. They were usually, a two-day meeting held at a major airport hub city for easy in and out. Once a year, however, the members would choose a resort hotel where they could extend their stay. These were typically held in the summer when members could bring their families and enjoy a mini vacation.

I spent eight years with two different NADA 20 groups from 1972 to 1980. Then in 1982, I joined a Nichols, Campbell & Marrow 20 Group. NCM was the firm that developed the original 20 group concept in 1947. At that time, NCM was a step up from my previous group with a more comprehensive program. It was also a step up when it came to selecting meeting locations.

I had been in the group for about three years when our summer/vacation meeting was held during an Alaskan Cruise on the Sun Princes. This was the end of July 1985. This was Joanne and my first time on a cruise ship. We spent a delightful 7 days on the Inland Passage, except for one scary incident.

One morning, while I was in the 20 group meeting, Joanne was in the lounge when a lady sitting next to her asked: "And where are you from?"

Joanne replied: "Cheyenne, Wyoming."

The other lady said: "I just heard on the radio that Cheyenne had a big flood!"

Joanne replied: "Oh no. That can't be right. It never floods in Cheyenne."

The date was August 2, 1985.

She immediately rushed to get me out of the meeting, and we spent the next several hours trying to get a ship-to-shore phone line to contact our children to make sure they were all right. We finally reached them, and everything was OK, but it was a scary several hours. We also checked on my mother who had already received some help from some dealership personnel and was doing fine.

The next day the Cheyenne newspaper's headlines read:

August 1, 1985, was one of the darkest days in Wyoming's history. A tragic flash flood in Cheyenne claimed 12 lives and caused over $60 million in property damage. The torrential storm rolled in with fury, dropping six inches of rain during the evening hours. The flooding created a deadly tidal wave that swept across the town.

NADA Conventions

Once a year, usually in February, the National Automobile Dealers Association holds its convention in a major metropolitan city. This is the premier marketplace for products, services, and technologies specifically tailored for the new-car dealership. 500 plus exhibitors put on displays with everything from large, fully assembled paint booths to the latest in sales follow-up programs and everything in between. They also put on workshops on many of the current topics of the day and many dealers bring their department heads to attend these informative classes.

Every manufacturer is represented and will typically put on a lavish evening cocktail reception for their dealers. GMAC has one of the largest receptions.

My parents would rarely miss a convention. Because it was held in February, Barbara and I would generally stay at home with a sitter. My parents would, however, on a few occasions, get us out of school for a week so we could take a mid-winter trip with them.

The earliest trip I remember the four of us taking was driving to the convention in Miami, Florida in 1951. We left a couple of days early because we had planned a side trip to Jacksonville, Florida to see the University of Wyoming Cowboys play in their first bowl game — The Gator Bowl.

The Wyoming fans were a big hit in Jacksonville. Many people had brought rolls of silver dollars to pay for their food and tips. Gambling, especially slot machines, was still legal in many Wyoming towns, and silver dollars were commonplace, but some Floridians had never seen one. We beat Washington & Lee 20-7.

Carl Sr. and Eleanor Halladay at the NADA Convention in Las Vegas 1968

The Legacy Continues

Jim Casey

The announcement was made at a press conference on March 12, 2020, that Jim Casey was now President and owner of Halladay Motors, Inc. Jim is the fourth dealer principal following Carl Sr., Carl Jr., and Tim Joannides to carry on the long tradition of the 80-year-old firm.

Jim's father was serving in the United States Air Force and was transferred to Warren Air Force Base in 1973. Jim entered sixth grade at Pioneer Park Elementary School. After finishing high school, he attended the University of Wyoming, studying Administration of Justice and Psychology.

Jim started his automotive career in Cheyenne selling cars for Bob Brunner Motors, Fassett-Nickel Ford and Bill Eger Ford in Denver. He returned to Fassett Nickel Ford as Finance and Insurance Manager and eventually became their General Sales Manager. He was then hired as Finance and Insurance Manager for Halladay Motors and served in that position from 1990 to 2000. Jim then took a job in Sheridan, Wyoming and spent the next six years as General Manager for the Toyota dealer there. Then in 2007, at Tim Joannides' request, Jim returned to Halladay Motors as General Sales Manager.

Tim Joannides saw Jim's potential and enrolled him in the NADA Dealership Management course that same year.

Jim and his wife, Heidi, found each other and married eleven years ago. They have three children, Taylor, Connor, and Jayme. Jim and Heidi live in North Cheyenne.

Jim Casey and Tim Joannides

After Jim Casey took the reins of the Halladay Auto Group, he immediately started researching the possibilities of building a new home for our rapidly growing Subaru line of cars. The ideal location, as it turned out, was right next door to the GM dealership. Many years earlier, we had purchased the adjacent vacant land with just this thought in mind.

In March of 2022, plans were being drawn up to build a new dealership facility. Between architects, builders, and Subaru, the state-of-the-art Halladay Subaru dealership building took shape at 2030 Westland Road and was completed in October 2023.

The New Subaru Building, 2030 Westland Road

The General Motors building got a complete upgrade and facelift in 2016.

The showroom was expanded to include some of the outdoor patio and a completely new service reception area was installed.

The new Halladay Auto Group now operates three of the most up-to-date, state-of-the-art dealership facilities in the Rocky Mountain area on Westland Road, Cheyenne, Wyoming.

Buick-GMC-Cadillac, Building
Upgrade, 2100 Westland Road

The Future

WHO KNOWS WHAT THE AUTOMOBILE INDUSTRY will look like in the next 100 years? No one could have predicted the changes that have occurred since my father started his dealership in 1944.

The view on the horizon indicates that we will have self-driving vehicles powered by something other than gasoline or diesel. Right now, it looks like electricity but in the future, it could be as exotic as some form of atomic fusion.

One thing is certain, and that is a quote from my father:

"People will always demand individual transportation!"

I am truly grateful to Tim Joannides and Jim Casey who have faithfully carried on My Father's Legacy.

Employee Loyalty and Longevity

OUR DEALERSHIP HAS ALWAYS BEEN a good place to work. Many employees have spent several years, and some have retired from Halladay Motors.

I would like to recognize a few long-time employees that I worked with. This is by no means a complete list and I apologize if I have left someone out.

Bill Huff celebrating his 41st anniversary with Jim Casey

Bill Huff – Reconditioning Manager – 45 years

Bob Ojeda – Body Shop Manager – 42 years -Retired

Joe Sanchez – Partsman – 40 years – Retired

Lee Tafoya – Salesman – 36 years – Retired.

Crist Lucero – Painter – 35 years – Retired.

Jose Vargas – Partsman, Parts Manager – 34 years – Retired.

Tom Ourada – Tire Dept. Mgr. – 28 years

Colt Anderson – Salesman – 28 years

Dick Adams – Service Mgr. – 27 years

Kathy Hayes – Office – 27 years

Andy Stiggers – Detail/Janitor – 25 years – Retired

Lee Willoughby – Salesman – 22 years – Retired.

John Lueras – Sales Manager – 21 years

Dyle Peters – Office Manager – 18 years – Retired.

The Halladay Automobile

IN 1993, A HUSBAND AND WIFE, Lawrence and Lil Halladay from Alberta, Canada, saw our highway billboard, stopped by the dealership, and asked for me. They shared with me information, articles, advertisements, and photos of the Halladay Automobile. This was the first time I had ever heard of a Halladay Automobile. Lawrence also shared with me photos of his fully restored 1910 Halladay.

About a year later another man and his wife, Jack and Linda Grimm from Kerrville, Texas were spending the summer in Loveland, Colorado and once again he saw one of our advertisements and called to meet. We agreed to have lunch and that next week Joanne and I would meet them at Poor Richards restaurant in Cheyenne. Jack informed us that he was the grandson of Louis Putnam Halladay, the man who had built the Halladay Automobile. Jack had spent his career as an MD in the US Air Force and had spent many years in search of a Halladay automobile.

A few years later Jack Grimm purchased the 1910 Halladay from Lawrence Halladay. They both invited me to come to see the car, but I never got that chance.

The Halladay Automobile was produced between 1905 and 1922. The original cars were built in Streator, Illinois, and after a change in ownership were produced by the new Halladay Motor Car Co. in Mansfield, Ohio with subsequent moves to Lexington, Attica, and Newark, Ohio. A 1910 Halladay served as a press car for the famous Glidden Automobile Tour and then in 1911, two Halladay Model 50 roadsters fared very well when participating in the Fifth Annual Reliability contest of the Chicago Motor Club.

My father, who had spent his whole life in the automobile business, never mentioned the Halladay Automobile. I never got the chance to ask him why and will never know the answer.

1912 Halladay Automobile

Yes, It was a right-hand drive.

About the Cover

THE COVER PHOTO is a copy of an oversized postcard that we used for years. Set in front of the dealership building we occupied for 22 years, "The busy 500 Block East Lincolnway." It features a 1959 Cadillac Eldorado Biarritz Convertible, a 1959 GMC Step-side Pickup Truck, a 1959 Oldsmobile 88 Convertible, and a 1959 Oldsmobile Dynamic 88 Fiesta Station Wagon. As close as I can tell, the black car in front of the Cadillac is a Hillman Husky. This was an English import that we were selling at that time.

Halladay Motors Postcard

Acknowledgments

I WOULD LIKE TO RECOGNIZE some people who helped bring this book to life: Wolf Design and Marketing, Richard Wolf (Consultant), Victoria Wolf (Cover and Interior Design), My Word Publishing, Polly Letofsky, Bobby Haas (Editor), Tim Joannides, Jim Casey, Jackie (Lueras) Meranda, Rick Durante, Al Benson, Bill Huff, Marsha Allen, Suzi Taylor, Ken Cina, and Mike Caswell.

About the Author

CARL HALLADAY JR. is a second-generation automobile dealer. After school and military service, he joined his father at the dealership, Halladay Motors, in Cheyenne Wyoming, and remained there until he retired in 2003. His father had many interesting stories about the 20 years he had spent with General Motors before coming to Cheyenne. Carl Jr. asked his father to put those stories on tape, and he did.

My Father's Legacy — The 80-Year History of Halladay Motors and the Four Owners Who Built It, is Carl Jr.'s first book and he's currently working on a second book about early automobile dealers.